PLANS OF ARCHITECTURE

HOUSE DETAILS

Author

Francisco Asensio Cerver

Editorial manager

Paco Asensio

Project coordinator

Ivan Bercedo (Architect)

Design and layout

Mireia Casanovas Soley

Translation & Proofreading

Amber Ockrassa

Photographers

Luis Godoa (*LE House*); Dennis Gilbert (*Check's House*); Bill Timmerman (*Burnette House*); Helene Bisnet (*House in Lincolnshine*); Eugeni Pons (*Margarida House*); Naito Architect & Assoc. (*House n. 14*); Hans Georg Tropper/Atelier Giencke (*House and workshop in Graz*); Nelson Kon (*Helio Olga House*); Todd Conversano (*Aronoff House*)

1998 ● Francisco Asensio Cerver   ISBN: 0-8230-7185-5   Printed in Spain

Published by:

Whitney Library of Design
an imprint of Watson and Guptill Publications/New York
1515 Broadway
New York-NY 10036 USA

All too often the distance between imagination and reality proves too great and the best ideas never see the light of day. When it is not for lack of funding or technical means, it is sometimes simply an overabundant mixture of ideas.

In the pages of *PA: house details* the factors which made a number of projects (namely, a group of single-family houses) into reality are studied. We have taken the constructive details, choice of materials and technical solutions to be as important as site distribution or facade composition in our treatment of these projects.

We have likewise included homes from diverse countries (United States, Brazil, Japan, Austria, Singapore, Mexico, England) with varying constructive systems that may seem familiar in their respective regions while being completely unknown in others.

A short text by the architects themselves prefaces each article. The plans are drawn to scale for easy measurement comparison. *Constructive details* come with a key in which each material is specified. Similarly, photographs have been chosen which augment the graphic documentation in order to better represent the look of the finished product.

This book, therefore, helps to bridge the gap between images and reality, the imagined and the achieved.

6/27/91
7:00pm

6-27

vertical cut

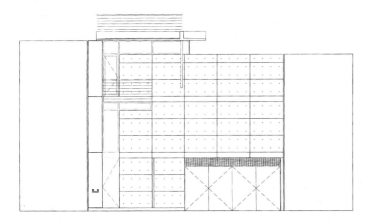

0   1   5m

STREET FACADE   (SECTION A–A)
FACHADA EXTERIOR (CORTE A–A)

Architect: *Taller de Arquitectura Enrique Norten Arquitectos S.C.*
(TEN Arquitectos)
Site: *Mexico D.F. (Mexico)*
Project Team: *Carlos Ordonez, Gustavo Espitia*
Major Material: *Walls of exposed concrete or concrete block with plaster.*
Patio facade of glazing. Louvers of red cider. Exposed steel
structure. Floors of lava stone and oak wood.
Structural Engineer: *Colinas and Buen Ingenieros,S.A.*
Square Footage: *3,200*

Facade facing the street.
Scale 1:200

View of the main facade. The house is
practically closed to the street. The
only two openings are a vertical strip
which leads from the entrance door to
the roof and a garage door.

A dense, urban residential area of town houses is the context for this single-family, three-story house. The site is a 32 x 55 foot slot of space sharing party walls with its neighbors, the short end of one of the continuous facades creates the defined street wall typical of this townhouse neighborhood. Jacaranda trees create a vault spanning the length of the street.

The architectural response to the project came from the orientation of the 1,800 square foot lot and the extreme compression of the space given. The site is divided in two along its longitudinal axis: a living block and an outdoor patio with an east-west orientation. Inserted between a high party wall and the interior facade, the patio space provides southern exposure to the house as well as privacy from the street and neighboring houses.

The principal living, dining and patio spaces are located on the middle floor, and connect to the bedrooms above and library below via a stair core at the rear of the house. The ground floor also contains the entry, garage, laundry, and service bedrooms. The roof of the house is utilized as a deck.

The size of the plot and the limited budget called for rational, straightforward organization. The house is a layering of slots of space, which run longitudinally along its full length on every level, and are transcribed onto the main facade. The first, a narrow layer of storage space which runs along the north wall is articulated as a smooth plane of wood. Parallel to this layer is the circulation of the house. The living spaces comprise the next wider zone, enclosed by a wall of glass which opens these spaces to the south. The southern sun is blocked by the deep overhang of the roof and the system of louvers in another plane parallel to the glass facade. Finally, the ivy of the south party wall creates a plane of green to contain and define the patio space.

The superimposition of layered slots of space creates transverse spatial relationships; the exterior spaces are referenced to the organization of the interiors. The living space is aligned with the void of the ground floor patio, while the kitchen block and dining space are coordinated with the patio of the first floor exterior dining room. The space of the library below is completed by the lower patio. Continuity of materials from exterior to interior create further spatial transparency between these two zones. The transparencies created by these interlocking volumes provide for various readings of the spaces.

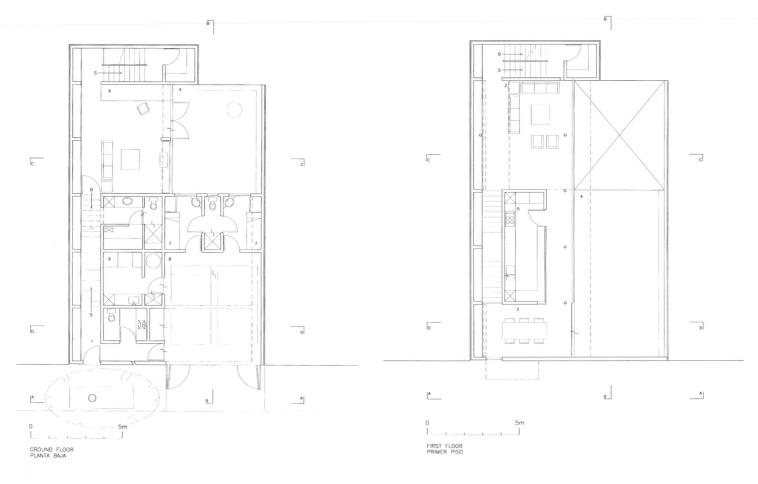

GROUND FLOOR
PLANTA BAJA

FIRST FLOOR
PRIMER PISO

0   5m

Ground floor. Scale 1:200

Second floor. Scale 1:200

1. Vestibule.
2. Living room.
3. Dining room.
4. Courtyard.
5. Kitchen.
6. Study.
7. Bedroom.
8. Garage.
9. Storage room.
10. Main bedroom.

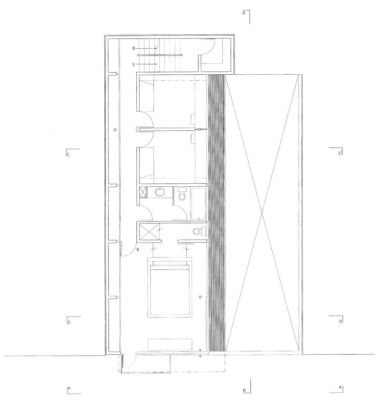

SECOND FLOOR
SEGUNDO PISO

0   5m

Third floor. Scale 1:200

View of the interior from the court-yard. The house and courtyard have almost the same surface. An interesting symmetry is created between the building and emptiness. Enrique Norten stresses that, in spite of the architect's obvious tendency to build, empty spaces are also rich and interesting.

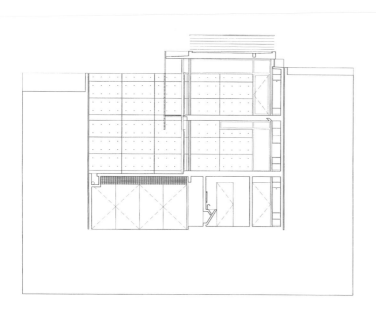

0 1   5m

SECTION D-D
CORTE D-D

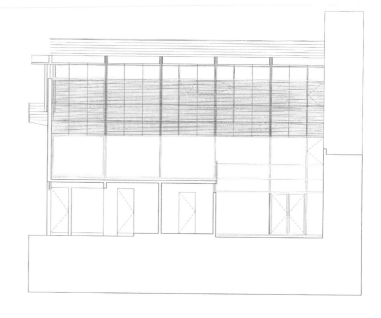

0 1   5m

INTERIOR FACADE (SECTION B-B)
FACHADA INTERIOR (CORTE B-B)

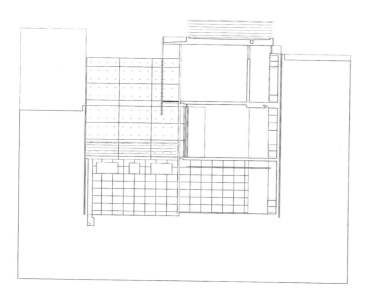

0 1   5m

SECTION C-C
CORTE C-C

Garage cross section. Scale 1:200

Rear study cross section. Scale 1:200

Longitudinal section. Scale 1:200

View of the courtyard.

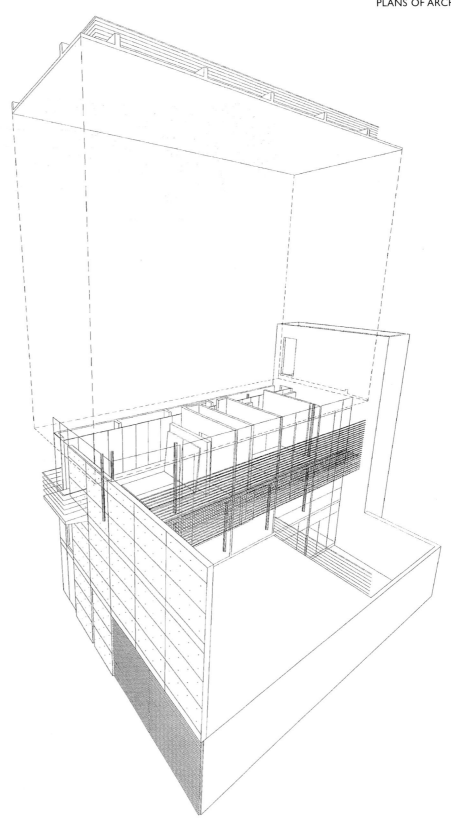

Axonometric projection. The house is as open to the courtyard as it is closed to the street. In this case, the exterior space is private, creating a richer relation between exterior and interior. The main facade separates the home from the courtyard. It is no ordinary separation, rather one around which the life of the house revolves. It produces a doubling of space on two stages: its actual location and its symmetrical counterpart, the courtyard.

On the third floor below the windows there is a small balcony protected by a lattice. It is a transition space between bedroom and courtyard which insures intimacy.

1. Cement whitewash.
2. 10 x 10 x 2cm bricks laid with cement and sand.
3. Waterproofing.
4. Layer of cement and sand.
5. Light filling.
6. Handrail.
7. Projection.
8. Point of light.
9. 50 x 20 cm x 1/4" steel plate anchored to slab stone.
10. 10cm. concrete slab with waterproofing.
11. Gutter.
12. Tie road cold-roll dia.1/2".
13. 10 cm. concrete slab.
14. Aluminum angles.
15. 3" x 3/4" red cedar strips. Natural varnish.
16. 6" metal column. Anti-corrosive paint. 3 coats of white, machine-applied lacquer.
17. Concrete.
18. 7.5cm. plinth of red oak.
19. Red oak parquet.
20. Leveling layer.
21. Plug.
22. Walkway.
23. 3" stainless steel supports attached to slab.
24. Irving aluminum grid.
25. 10cm. concrete slab.
26. Point of light.
27. 7.5cm. plinth of red oak.
28. 4"x 2½" aluminum carpentry. 6mm. glass.
29. Red oak parquet.
30. Leveling layer.
31. 12cm. concrete slab.
32. 60 x 40 x 2 black American stone.
33. Mortar.
34. Waterproofing.
35. Concrete step.
36. Steel lattice.
37. 12cm. concrete slab.
38. Lighting box
39. Plaster and paint.
40. Polished cement.
41. Cement block.
42. Fluorescent light.
43. Mirror over pine frame.
44. Concrete.
45. Drainage.
46. 7.5cm. plinth of red oak.
47. Reinforced concrete with 10 x 10 cm. welded mesh.
48. Layer of cement.
49. Waterproofing.

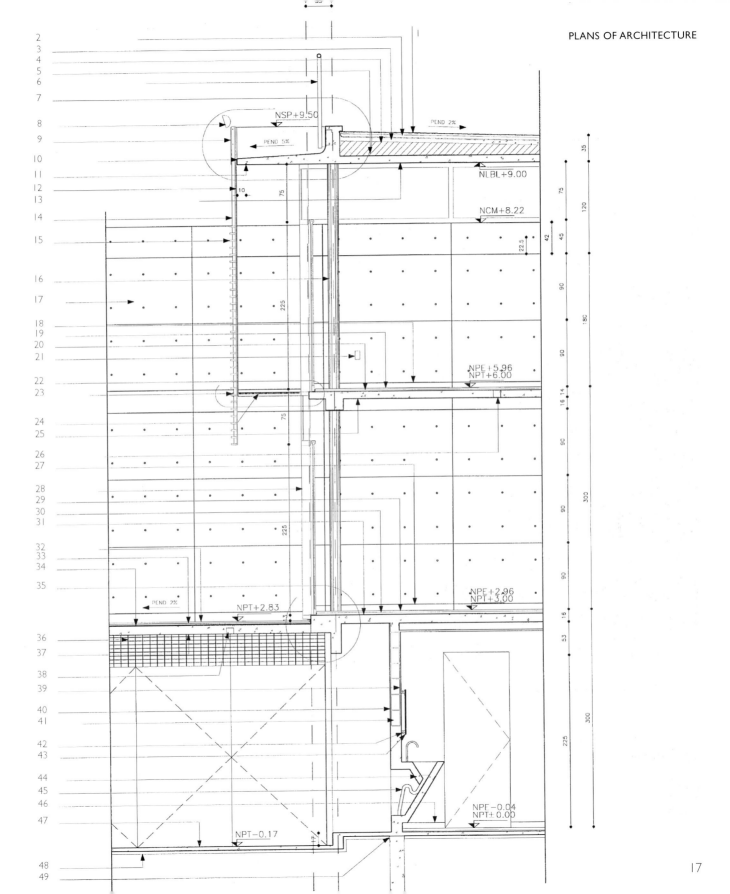

Window detail on the third floor of the facade facing the street.

1. Handrail.
2. 300 w lamp.
3. 10cm. concrete slab.
4. Iron plate of 8 cm.1/4" diameter.
5. Round Cold-Roll, diameter 1/2"
6. Iron plate, 50X20cm. 1/4"
7. Aluminum angles.
8. Red cedar strips.
9. Steel column.
10. Aluminum grid.
12. 4 X 2½" aluminum carpentry.
    9 mm. glass.
13. Built-in plate to receive column.
14. Handrail.
15. Black American stone plinth built into the wall.
16. Black American stone.
17. Waterproofing.
18. 12cm. concrete slab.
19. Lattice.
20. Lattice
21. Cement finish.
22. Automatic door. Iron sheet, anti-corrosive paint, enamel.
23. View of the door.
24. Iron angle.
25. Reinforced concrete floor with 10 X 10cm. welded mesh.

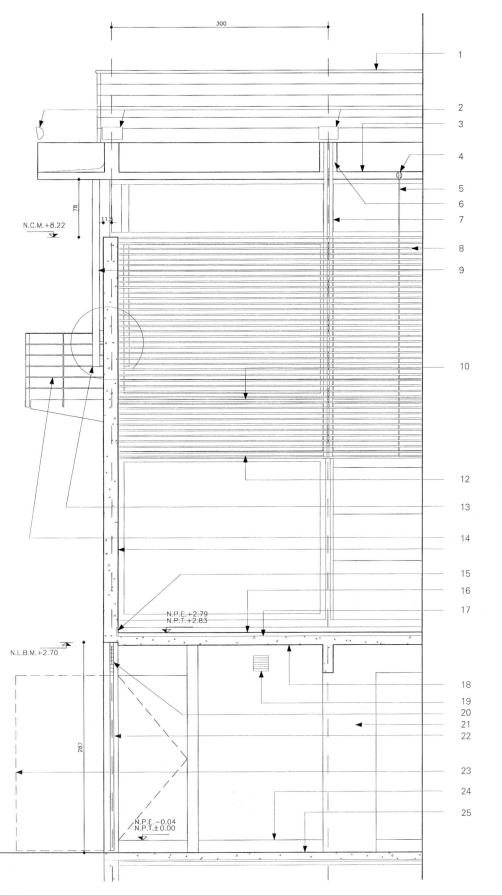

300

78

N.C.M.+8.22

N.P.E.+2.79
N.P.T.+2.83

N.L.B.M.+2.70

287

N.P.E.−0.04
N.P.T.±0.00

1
2
3
4
5
6
7
8
9
10
12
13
14
15
16
17
18
19
20
21
22
23
24
25

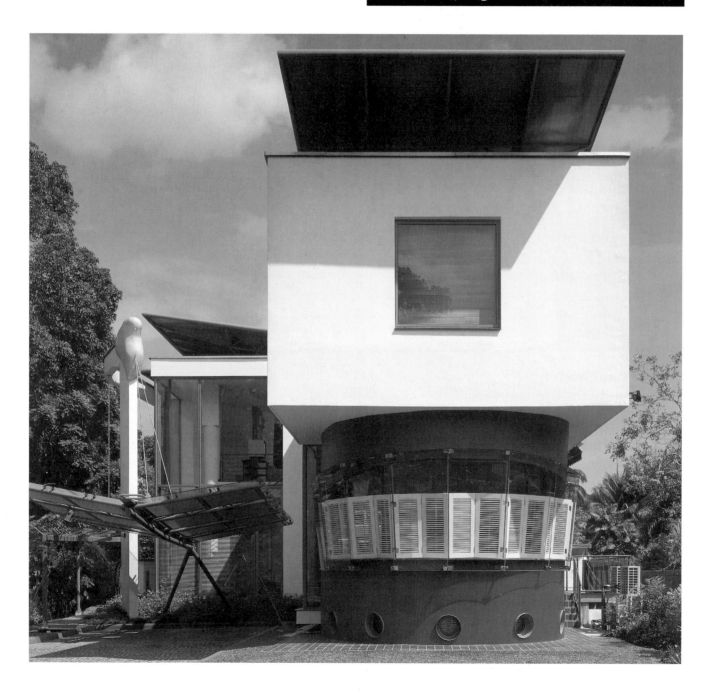

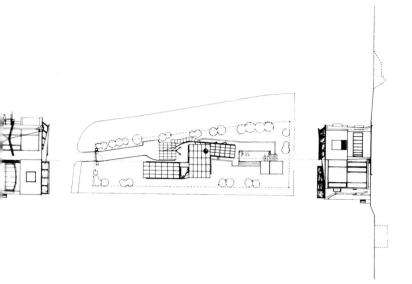

Architect: *KNTA Architects*
Kay Ngee Tan, Teck Kiam Tan
Site: *Singapore*
Structure: *Joseph Huang, Ove Arup & Partners-Singapore*
Specialist Contractors: *Ho Kong Aluminium Pte. Ltd;*
Xin Hefen Engineering Pte. Ltd.

The site on which Check House is located is clearly longitudinal, which is reflected in the design of the house and the gardens. The spaces are linked to each other in a dynamic succession of volumes in continuous dialogue. On the ground floor, the forms are fluid and curvilinear, while on the first floor they become straight and angular, forming independent bodies.

The house is conceived as a sequence of stages in which the places succeed each other naturally.

A small cobbled drive allows cars to reach the house, crossing the front garden. The entrance is located right in the center of the house, at the point of inflection of the gentle curve of the ground floor plan. A curved ramp gives access to the entrance from the parking zone, dominated by the sculptural image of a pergola suspended from a stay on one of its sides.

After the entrance door, continuing the eastern tradition, an illuminated semicircular screen has been placed: the light does not go through the screen but is reflected by it.

All the elements of the house converge at the living room, a double height space. The views open onto both the front and rear gardens, where the pool is located. This is an open space, surrounded by large windows. To the west, an oblique wall protects the house from the last rays of sun, and allows enjoyment of the tropical garden that surrounds the house.

The dining room is located beside the front garden. It is a circular room that has been designed around a central round table for twelve persons.

At the north end of the house, near the pool, a small pavilion has been added with glass blocks and a roof of two overhanging eaves supported on a single girder.

The walls, built in concrete, form the basic structure of the house. The various elements made with other materials are anchored or suspended by its edge from the end of a girder overhanging the building. Under the upper glass roof that provides protection from the rain, perforated steel panels have been placed.

A light glass roof, suspended from an exposed girder at the perimeter and separated from the facade on the east side, provides weather protection. Also, to protect the concrete roof of the house from the sun, a second matte anodised aluminium roof has been built.

The spaces of this house are created to be enjoyed, and for this reason the freedom with which they were designed is contagious.

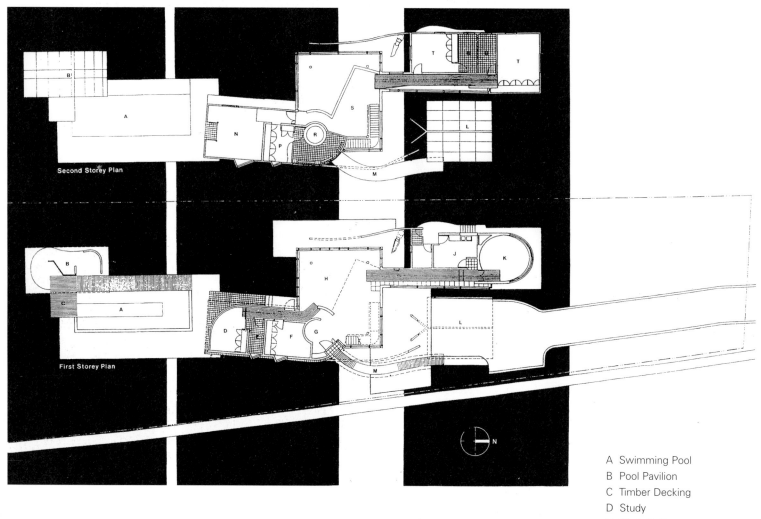

Second Storey Plan

First Storey Plan

A Swimming Pool
B Pool Pavilion
C Timber Decking
D Study
E Study Bathroom
F Guest Bathroom
G Entrance Hall
H Living Room
K Dining Room
L Carporch
M Pedestrian Walkway
N Master Bedroom
P Dressing Room
R Master Bathroom
S Family Room
T Bedroom
U Bathroom

The site on which Check House is located is clearly longitudinal, which is reflected in the design of the house and the gardens.
On the ground floor, the forms are fluid and curvilinear, while on the first floor they become straight and angular, forming independent and identifiable bodies.

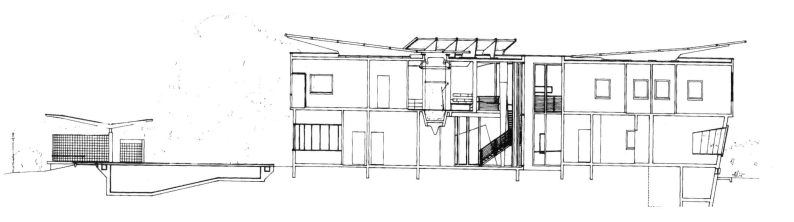

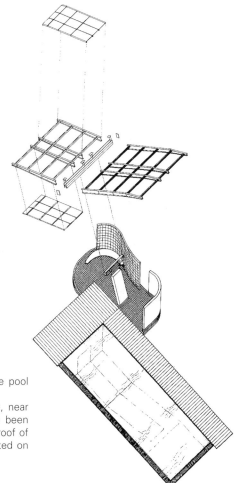

In addition to reducing the effect of sunlight, the double roof is one of the elements of greatest visual impact.

Construction axonometry of the pool and the adjacent pavilion.
At the north end of the house, near the pool, a small pavilion has been added with glass blocks and a roof of two overhanging eaves supported on a single girder.

Construction details of the canopy.

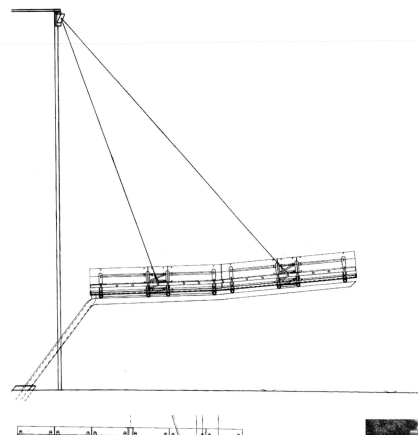

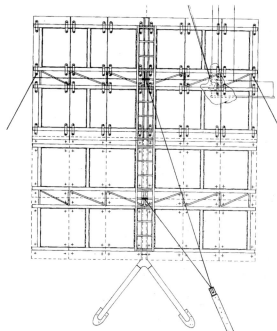

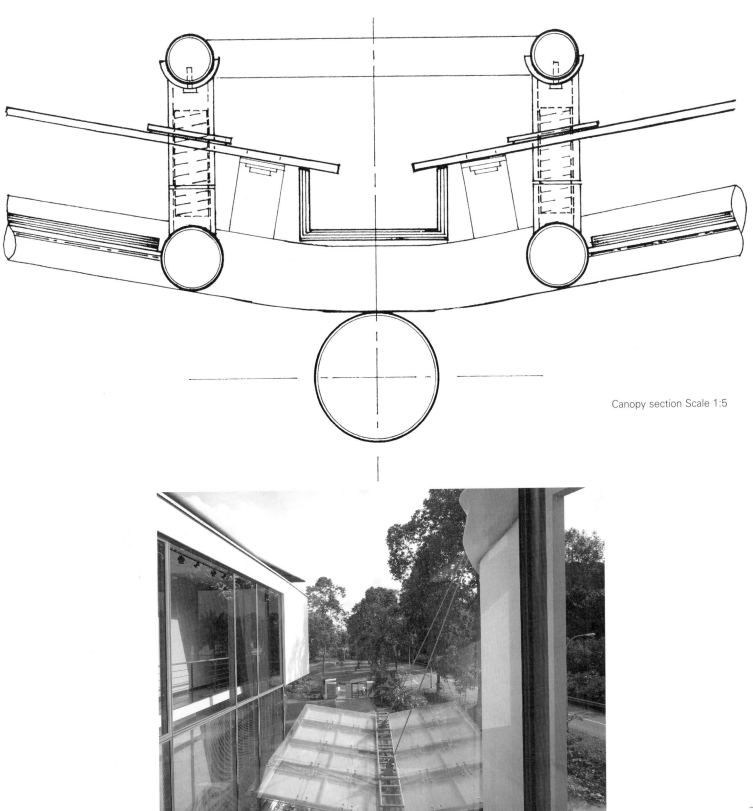

Canopy section Scale 1:5

The anchoring of the canopy incorporates an anecdotic element in the composition of the facade.

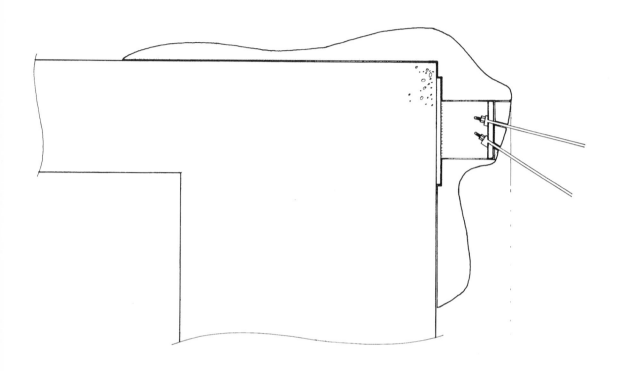

On the following page:

A light glass roof, suspended from an exposed girder at the perimeter and separated from the facade on the east side, provides weather protection for the path that goes from the garden to the pool at the rear of the house.

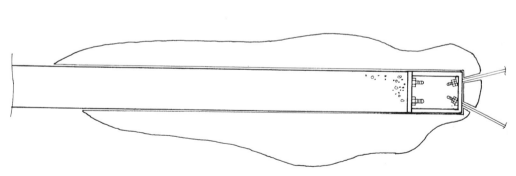

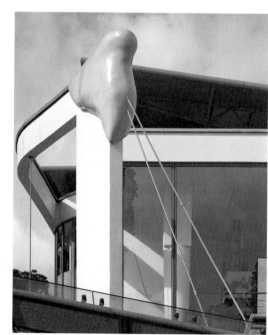

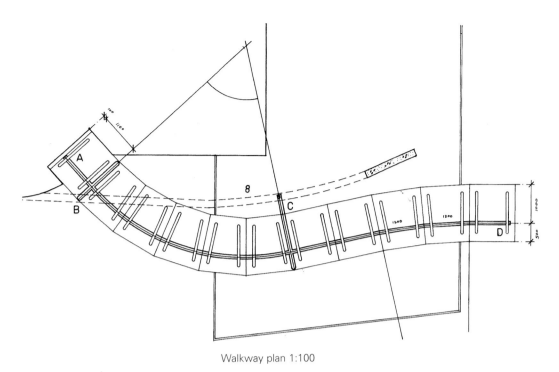

Walkway plan 1:100

Pedestrian canopy

1. 100 x 150 x 5 RHS.
2. 50 x 5 along plate whole length.
3. 12 mm baseplate & 4 x M 16 hold-
   ing-down bolts to concrete footing.
4. Concrete footing.
5. 5 x 114 dia. CHS.
6. 75 x 20 s/s support & 50 x 10 s/s
   stiffener plate.
7. 25 dia. cable rod.
8. RC tie-beam.
9. Hilti HEA capsule.
10. 5 mm thick dark blue fibreglass,
    silicone jointed.
11. S/s fixing.
12. 25 x 125 external quality kapor
    planks s/s nailed onto timber packing.
13. New landscape up to walkway
    level.

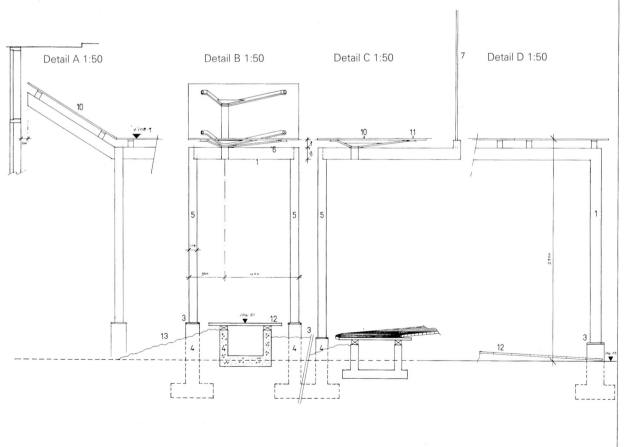

Detail A 1:50   Detail B 1:50   Detail C 1:50   Detail D 1:50

27

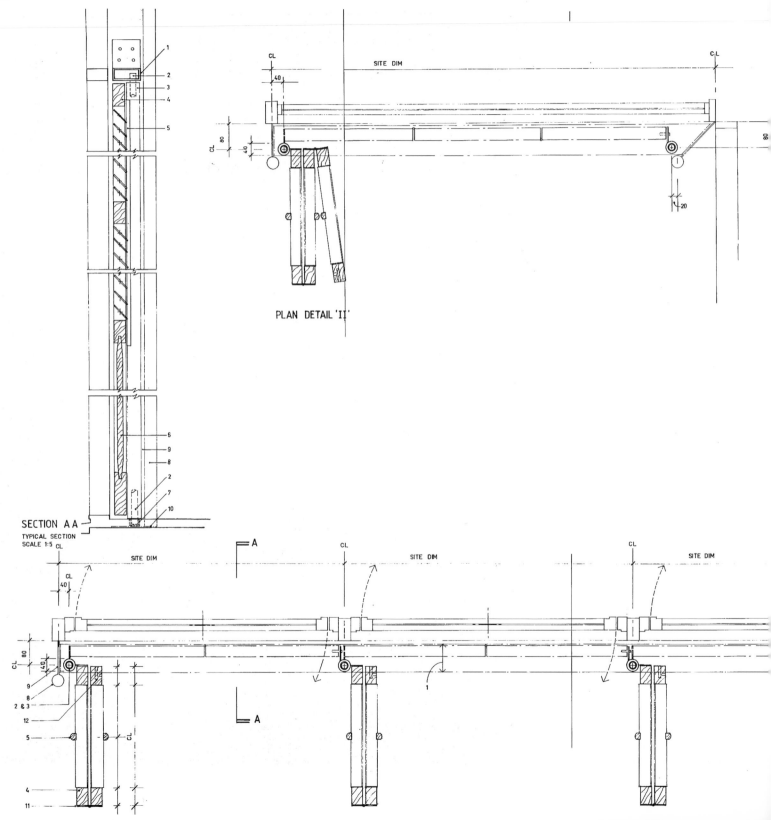

PLAN DETAIL 'II'

SECTION A A

TYPICAL SECTION
SCALE 1:5

SITE DIM

Living room shutters detail, scale 1/30

1. 90x40mm-steel rectangular section holding vertical pivots for shutters.
2. Inner pivot rod of stainless steel. (aprox D20-25mm). Continuous rod from floor socket to fixing in top rail.
3. Mild steel outer tube cut into equal sections of approx. 200 mm long.
4. Timber frame (nyatoh or similar)
5. Adjustable louvres and adjusting rod attached.
6. Timber infill panel with white paint finish.
7. Stainless steel floor socket to receive rod.
8. Rod welded to steel fin of main window frame.
9. Fin structure of main window frame
10. Base plate to fin of main window structure.
11. Timber shutters hinged together with four hinges at regular intervals.
12. Key operated deadlock to suit timber shutter frame.

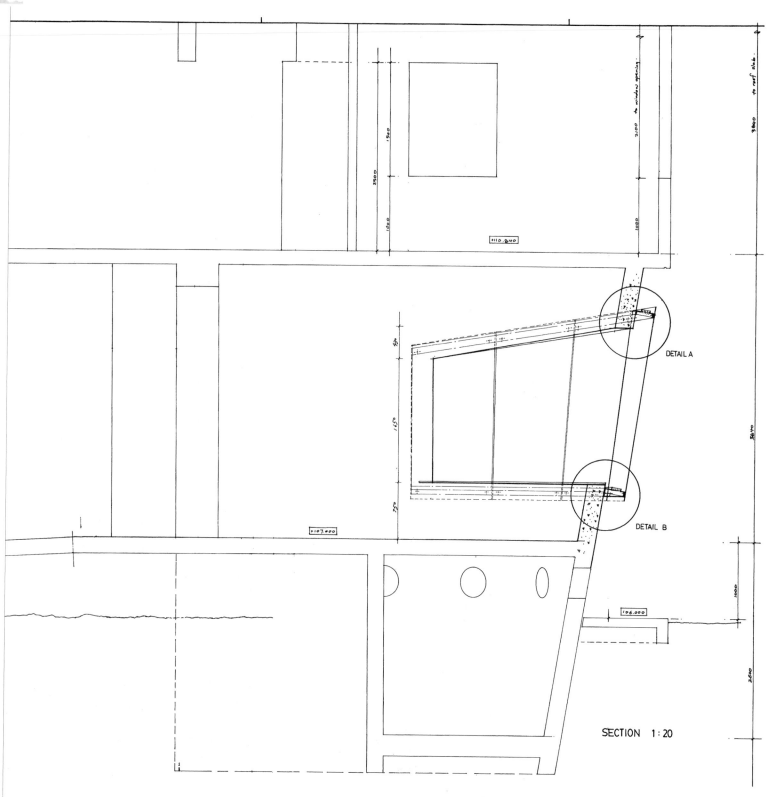

DETAIL A

DETAIL B

SECTION 1:20

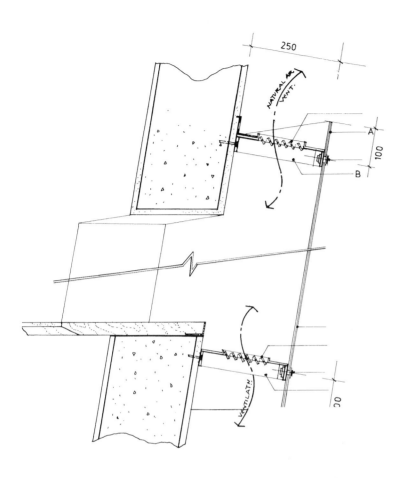

250

100

A

B

NATURAL AIR VENT.

VENTILAT.N.

A. 10 or 12 mm strengthened glass
B. Aluminium or stainless steel
   support, 4-6mm thick, fixed
   onto the external wall with stainless
   steel crews
C. Adjustable ventilation louvres of
   stainless steel
D. Stainless steel bolt

Detail of dining room
window. Scale 1:10

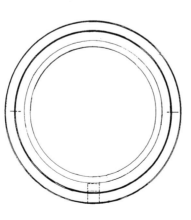

Elevation

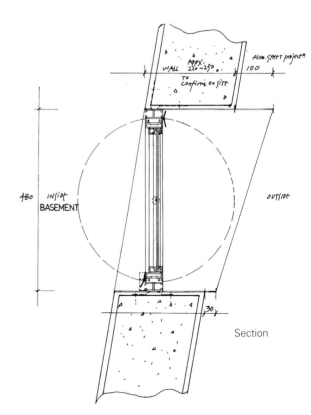

WALL
APPX.
250~250
To confirm on site

Alum. sheet projectn
100

480   INSIDE
BASEMENT

OUTSIDE

30

Section

31

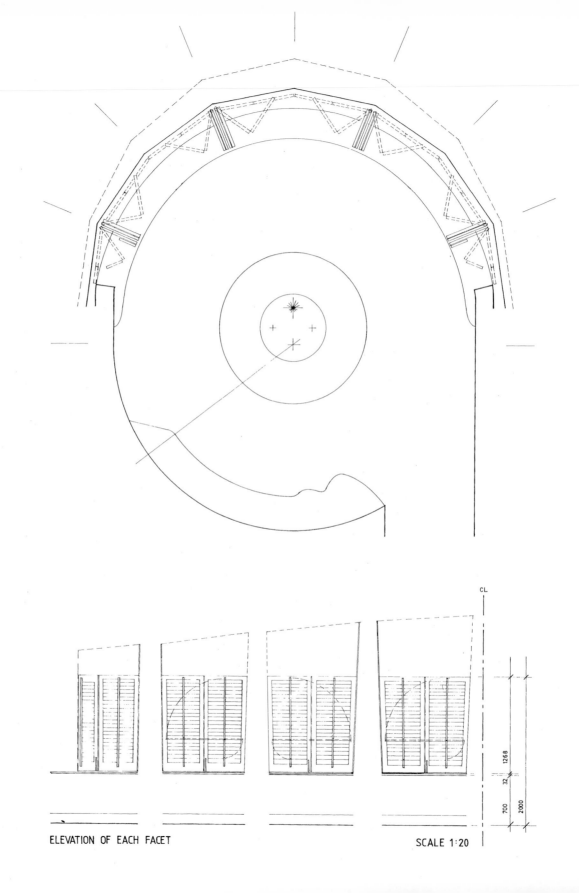

ELEVATION OF EACH FACET

SCALE 1:20

1268

32

700

2000

CL

Dining room shutters.

1. Nyatoh timber shutter with adjustible louvre section
2. Lever rod to adjust the louvres.
3. Bolt to hold louvres in open position
4. Predrilled hole with satin stainless steel finish inserted flush with wood surface.
5. Solid nyatoh cill 32 mm thick with edge profile as drawn
6. Steel bracket to support pivot /hinge for shutter.
7. Stainless steel rod
8. Custom made steel hinges for shutters.
9. Washers and nuts to screw onto end and rod. Designed by contractor to architects approval

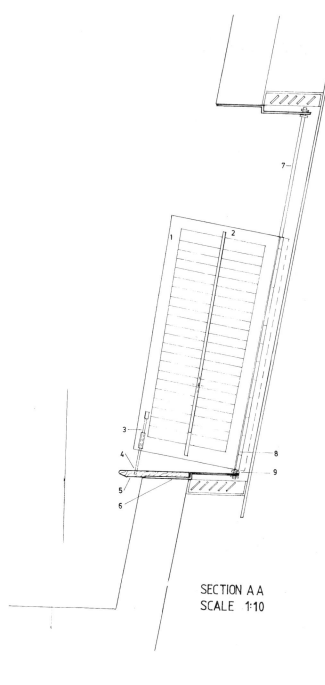

SECTION A A
SCALE 1:10

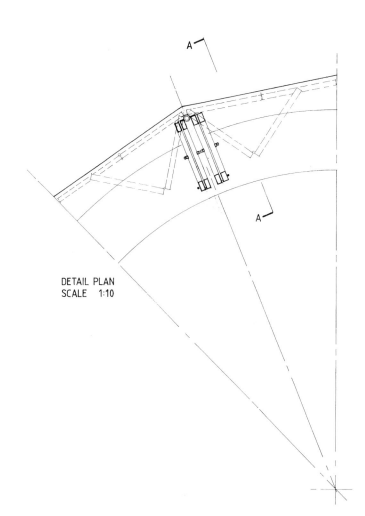

DETAIL PLAN
SCALE 1:10

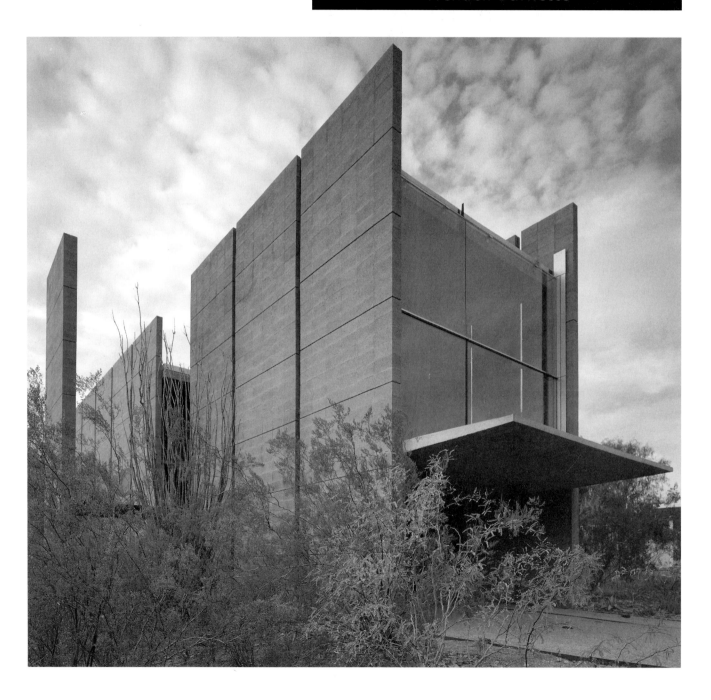

Architect: *Wendell Burnett*
Site: *Sunnyslope, Arizona (USA)*
Structural Engineer: *Caruso Turley and Scott Consulting Structural Engineer*
Mechanical Engineer: *Otterbein Engineering*
Landscape Design: *Burnette Landscape Design*
Square Footage: *1,160*
Major Exterior Materials: *Masonry (8 x 8 x 16 stacked bond "integra") and Glass (1" insulated glass w/ low-E on surface 3, w/ Solex exterior light).*
Cost: *$ 120,000*

The design solution is like a "Band-Aid" for the scar; a man-made canyon that renders the surrounding neighborhood less visible- focusing the view and creating a sense of isolation from the desert mountains to the east. An internal court allows natural light to penetrate the 92' structure bar, providing a moment of focus within the canyon. From the auto and pedestrian entry, the internal garden is the focus, an oasis of light, shade and water, which has acces to the separate interior volumes and living spaces that lie above and below. This vertical movement culminates with a clear acrylic plunge pool suspended in mid-a0ir by stainless steel cable rendering the court with refracted light in an endless change of drama. The pool is accessed by a sky-bridge that connects the ocean liner like roof terraces which capture 360 degree views of sunrise/sunset and the city grid of lights at night.

Parallel rows of post-tensioned cantilevered masonry monoliths act as stilts allowing in-situ concrete slabs to simply span the house's 16' width and float above the natural slope minimazing costly mountain site excavation. The R-28 monoliths are separated by continuously vertical 6'' wide glass slots. 8' wide monoliths are utilized on the south elevation rendering a massing that allows minimum penetration of south light into the interior. In contrast, the north elevation utilizes 4' wide monoliths rendering a strikingly different massing that allows maximum penetration of north light.

A fully shaded evaporative pool below the studio floor emits water via a trough similar to a desert canyon seep, down the natural slope of the site creating a micro-climate in the internal court enhancing cross ventilation. High efficency heat pumps provide for heating and cooling during extremes.

A series of cantilevered glass walls create an entry corridor and courts by day and a primary colors sculptures by night. Moonlight blue envelopes the suspended pool and floods up from the ground at the 6'' glass slots rendering the north and south elevations distinct.

Sketch of section in which solar ray
intensity is studied.

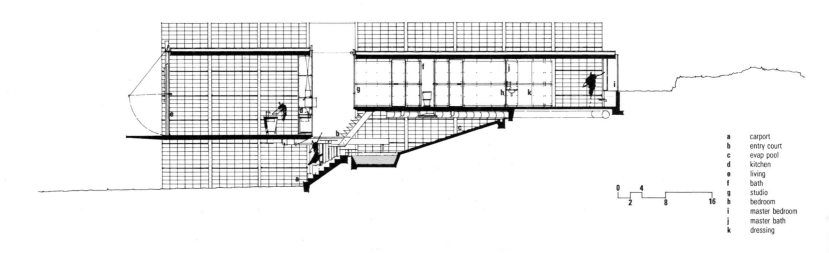

a	carport
b	entry court
c	evap pool
d	kitchen
e	living
f	bath
g	studio
h	bedroom
i	master bedroom
j	master bath
k	dressing

Cross section.

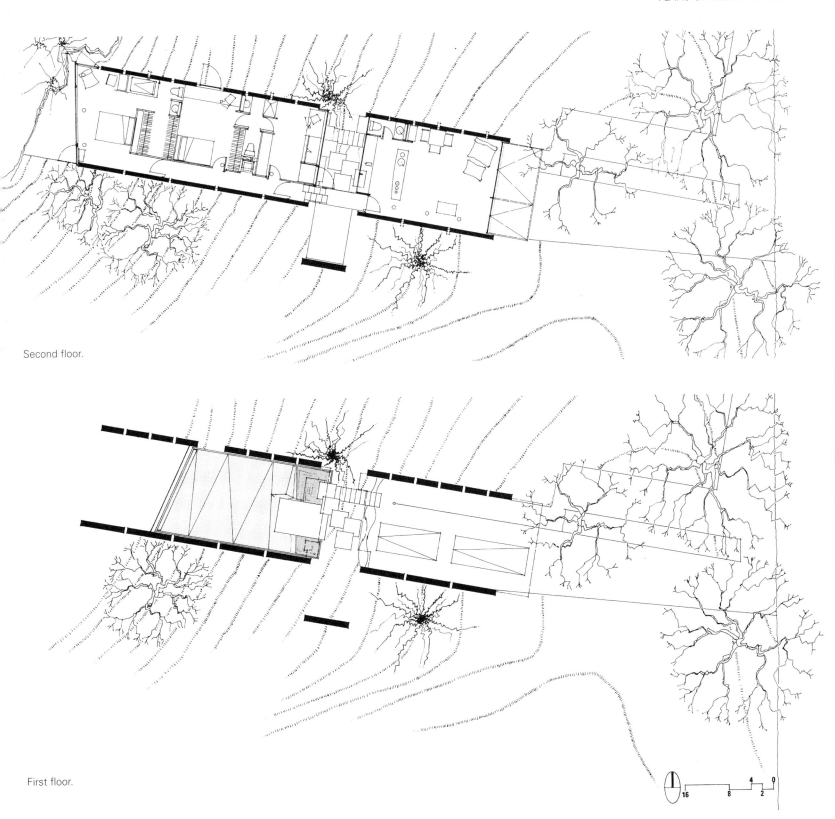

Second floor.

First floor.

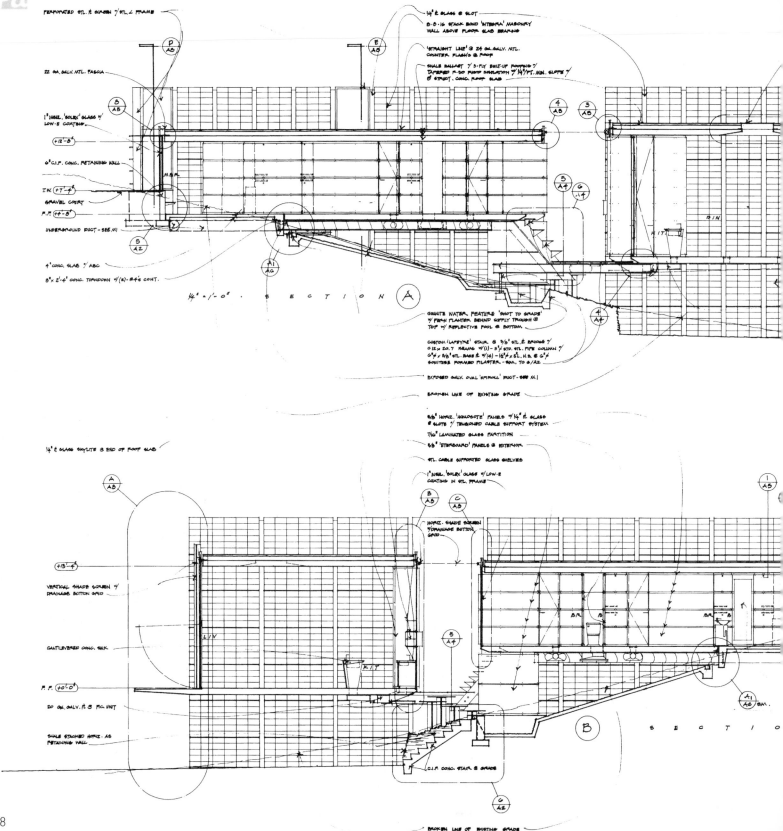

PERFORATED STL. SCREEN ON STL. C FRAME

1/4" GLASS @ SLOT

8·8·16 STACK BOND 'INTEGRA' MASONRY
WALL ABOVE FLOOR SLAB BEARING

'STRAIGHT LINE' @ 24 GA. GALV. MTL.
COUNTER FLASH'G @ ROOF

SHALE BALLAST ON 3-PLY BUILT-UP ROOFING ON
TAPERED R-30 ROOF INSULATION 1/4"/FT. MIN. SLOPE ON
8" STRUCT. CONC. ROOF SLAB

22 GA. GALV. MTL. FASCIA

1" INSUL. 'SOLEX' GLASS ON
LOW-E COATING

+12'-8"

6" C.I.P. CONC. RETAINING WALL

T.W. +7'-4"

GRAVEL COURT

F.F. +4'-8"

UNDERGROUND DUCT - SEE M1

4" CONC. SLAB ON ABC

8" x 2'-4" CONC. TURNDOWN ON (2)-#4's CONT.

1/4"=1'-0"   S E C T I O N A

GUNITE WATER FEATURE 'SHOT TO GRADE'
ON FRCH PLANTER BEHIND SUPPLY TROUGH @
TOP ON REFLECTIVE POOL @ BOTTOM

CUSTOM 'LABEYRIE' STAIR @ 5/8" STL. BRIDGE ON
C 12 x 20.7 BEAM'G ON (1) STD. STL. PIPE COLUMN ON
6"ø x 5/8" STL. BASE R ON (4)-1/2"ø x 5" H.B. @ 6" ON
GUNITE FORMED PILASTER - EQ. TO 8/A2

EXPOSED GALV. OVAL 'SPIROLL' DUCT - SEE M1

BROKEN LINE OF EXISTING GRADE

5/8" HORIZ. 'HOMOSOTE' PANELS ON 1/4" GLASS
@ SLOTS ON TENSIONED CABLE SUPPORT SYSTEM

7/16" LAMINATED GLASS PARTITION

5/8" 'ETHERBOARD' PANELS @ EXTERIOR

STL. CABLE SUPPORTED GLASS SHELVES

1" INSUL. 'SOLEX' GLASS ON LOW-E
COATING IN STL. FRAME

1/4" GLASS SKYLITE @ END OF ROOF SLAB

HORIZ. SHADE SCREEN
ON DRAINAGE BOTTOM
GRID

+13'-4"

VERTICAL SHADE SCREEN ON
DRAINAGE BOTTOM GRID

CANTILEVERED CONC. SINK

F.F. +10'-0"

20 GA. GALV. R @ FIG. UNIT

SHALE STACKED HORIZ. AB
RETAINING WALL

B   S E C T I O N

C.I.P. CONC. STAIR @ GRADE

BROKEN LINE OF EXISTING GRADE

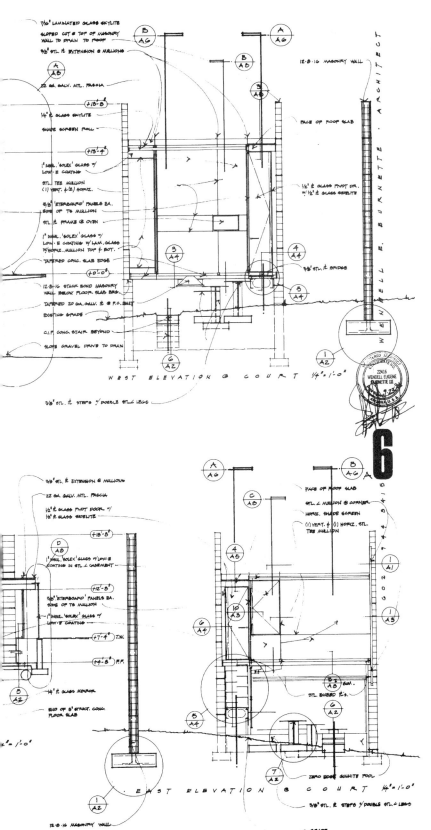

Construction layouts.

Detail of side wall.

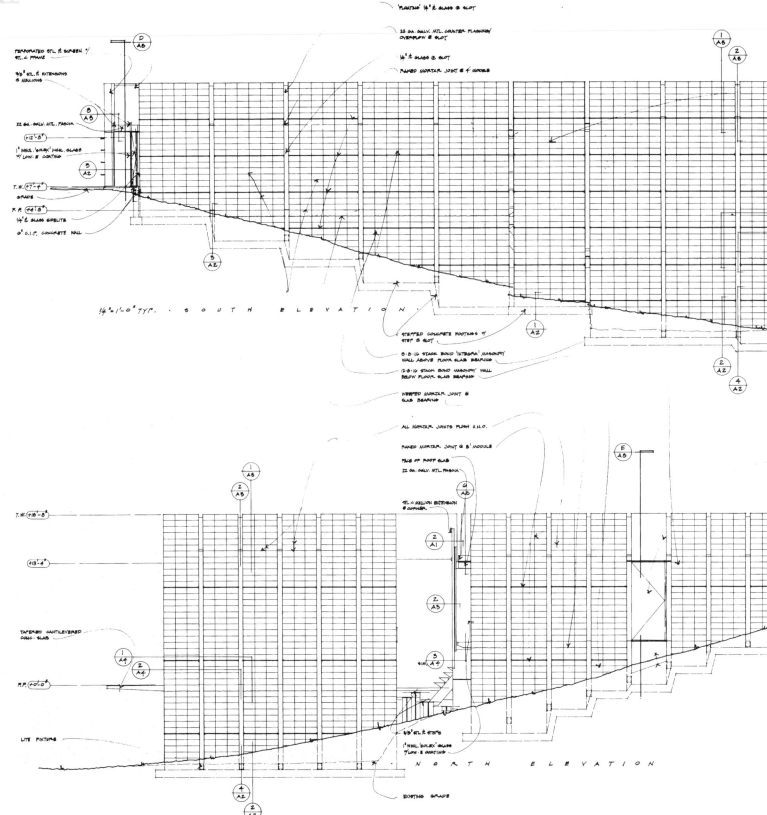

14"=1'-0" TYP. · S O U T H   E L E V A T I O N

N O R T H   E L E V A T I O N

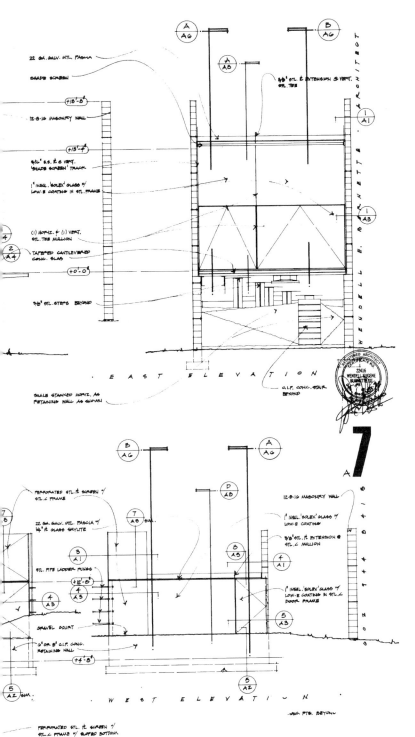

Lateral walls of concrete are completely blind. Light reaches the interior through vertical slots between wall sections. Thus, the house is nearly hermetically sealed except for the walls. At night, the slots become vertical illuminated stripes.

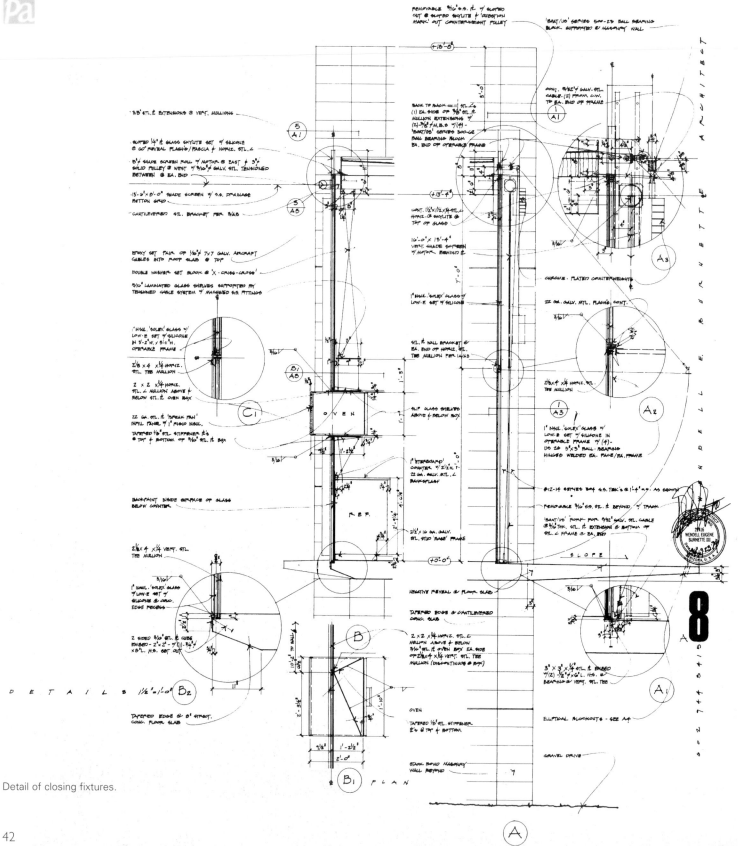

Detail of closing fixtures.

House in Lincolnshire

Caruso/St. John

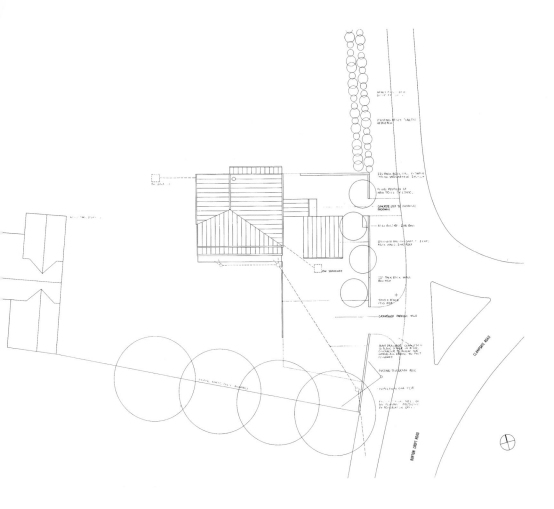

Architects: *Adam Caruso and Peter St.John*
Site: *Lincolnshire (U.K.)*
Structural Engineers: *Alan Baxter and Associates*

Site plan.

View of north facade. In spite of the house's traditional look, closer scrutiny of windows and construction details reveals its very modern character. In this sense, it has certain traits in common with houses by Jacobsen or Aalto.

One thing is clear, British architects are now looking for new directions. There is currently no single issue, no major controversy, no particular style that motivates creative action. This house for a couple at the edge of a small village in Lincolnshire is a perfect example.

This design sets out to articulate the threshold between the village and the large scale of the fenlands beyond, in a house that provides a set of related and generous spaces.

The square plan and dome-like shape of the roof make a place in the expanse of the Fenlands. The main living space is conceived as a "hall" around which are gathered the kitchen and bedrooms, all under a vaulted roof. The plan is compact, providing generous social spaces within a limited floor area.

The house has a facetted shape, higher towards the distant views to the north and lower to the garden. The window openings are made with galvanised steel frames which cover the surface of the brick wall, to give the brickwork the quality of a veneer.

The resulting volume takes its place within the simple and direct character of the buildings of the agricultural landscape.

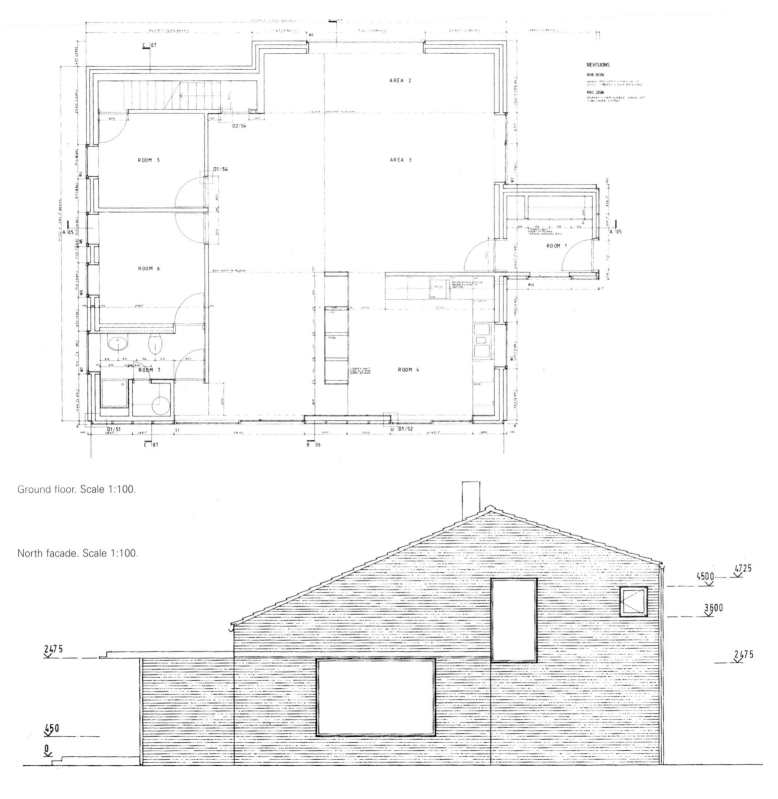

Ground floor. Scale 1:100.

North facade. Scale 1:100.

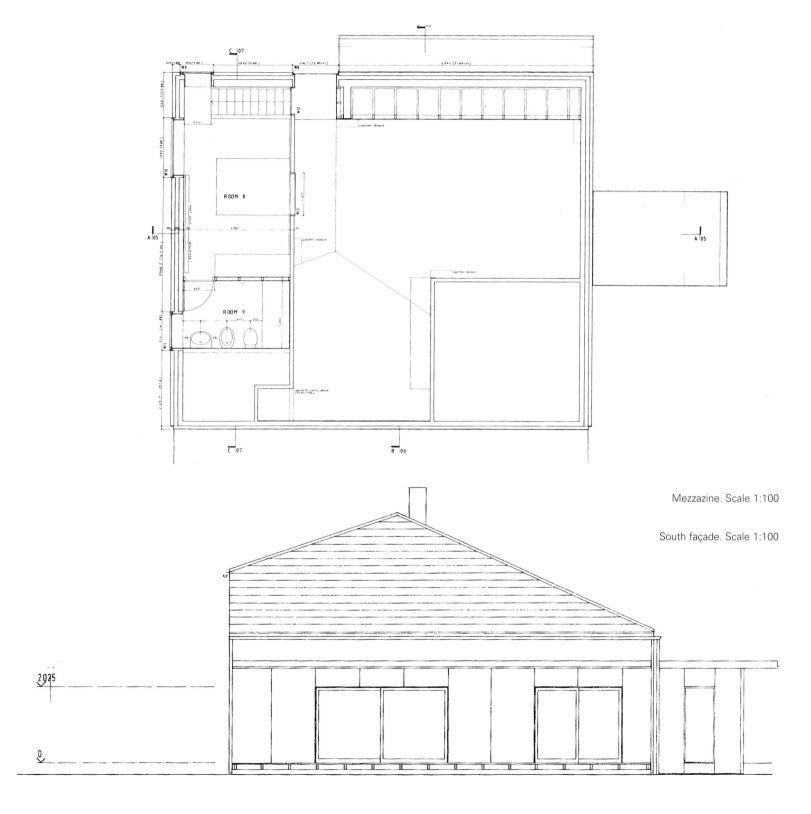

Mezzazine. Scale 1:100

South façade. Scale 1:100

East facade. Scale 1:100.

2025

900

0

1350

675

E A S T   E L E V A T I O N

West facade. Scale 1:100.

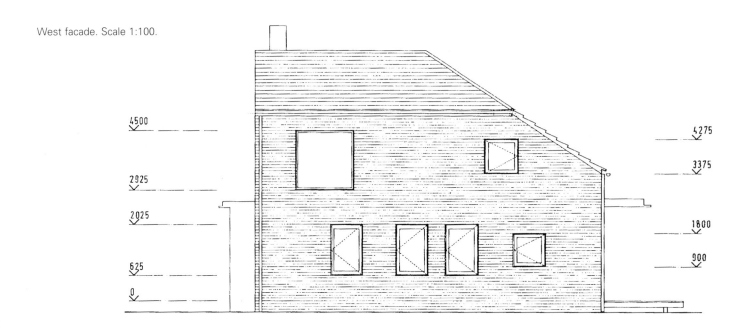

4500

2925

2025

625

0

4275

3375

1800

900

W E S T   E L E V A T I O N

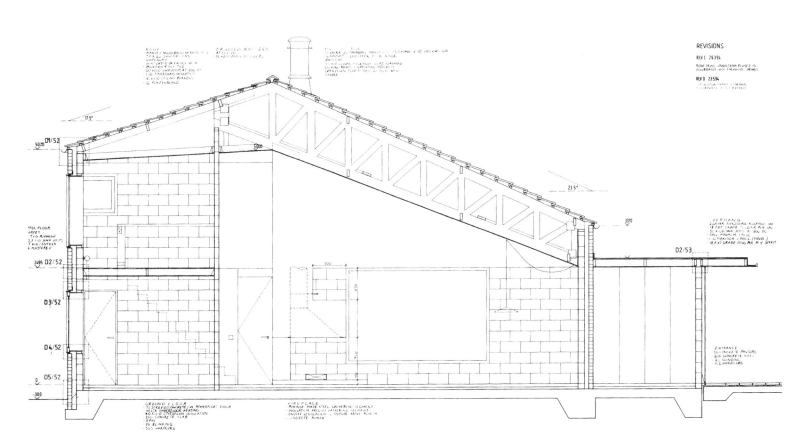

REVISIONS

REV C 26394

ROOF TRUSS CONNECTIONS REVISED IN
ACCORDANCE WITH ENGINEERS DRAWINGS

REV D 23594

Section AA. Scale 1:50

49

View of living room. Fittings, such as the closet separating the kitchen from the dining room or the fireplace, have been designed by the architects themselves. The floor is polished concrete. Wood pieces combine different tones.

Section BB. Scale 1:50

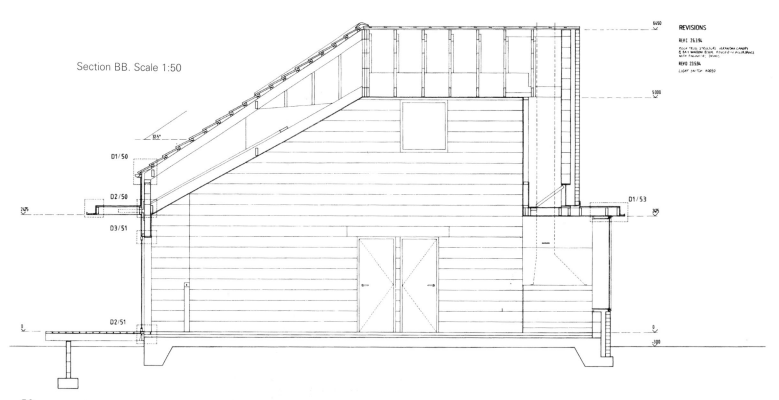

Construction detail of the
west facade. Scale 1:10

ROOF
· MARLEY 'MODERN' CONCRETE TILE ON
38 x 25 SWD BATTENS ON
UNDERLAY ON
50 x 150 RAFTERS ON 600 OC
· CONTINUOUS VENTILATOR FIXED TO
TOP OF BRICK
· MARLEY 'PREMIER' GUTTER AND
RW FITTINGS

CEILING
· 12.5 PLASTERBD W.
3 SKIM COAT (EDGE BEADS)
50 x 125 BEARERS
150 FIBREGLAS INSULATION

FIRST FLOOR
· CARPET ON
18 T+G PLYWOOD ON
50 x 150 JOISTS AT 600 OC
12.5 PLASTERBD W.
3 SKIM COAT (W. EDGE BEADS)

EXTERNAL WALL
· 100 BRICK
· 100 CAVITY W.
45 STYROFOAM RIGID INSULATION
· 140 CONCRETE BLOCK, FAIRFACED
(100, 200 CONCRETE BLOCK AS SHOWN
ON PLANS 107/03, 04)

OPENING WINDOW
· PROPRIATARY STEEL LINTOL BUILT
INTO BRICK JAMBS.
· P.C. CONCRETE LINTOL, FULL BLOCK HEIGHT
BUILT INTO INTERNAL FAIRFACED WALL
· DPC AS SHOWN, CODE 4 LEAD FLASHING
DRESSED OVER STEEL WINDOW FRAME.

· 50 x 75 x 6 GALV. RSA FRAME FIXED TO
BRICK JAMBS W. CSK ANCHOR BOLTS
(TOP ANGLE OF FRAME: 50 x 100 x 6 GALV. RSA)

· DOUG. FIR OPENING FRAME W.
6·6·6 SEALED UNIT, CLEAR FLOAT
GLASS BOTH PANELS
· GLAZED W. SLOTTSEAL E PROFILE SYSTEM
BOTTOM BEADS TO HAVE DRAINAGE SLOTS.

REVEAL
· 15 + 30 MDF, AS SHOWN, ON
SWD GROUNDS.

GROUND FLOOR
· 75 CONCRETE FLOOR W. A142 MESH
POWERFLOAT FINISH, BUTTED EXPANSION
JOINTS AS SHOWN ON PLAN 107/03
· VELTA UNDERFLOOR HEATING WITHIN 75 THICKNESS
· 40 STYROFOAM RIGID INSULATION
· 200 CONCRETE RAFT W. A142 MESH
· HEAVY DUTY POLYTHENE DPM
25 BLINDING LAYER
HARDCORE

EXTERNAL WALL
BURTON CROFT ROAD
CARUSO ST JOHN ARCHITECTS
071 609 9277

SCALE 1:5
DRWG: 107/52

D1

D2

D3

D4

D5

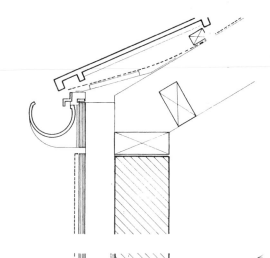

ROOF
- MARLEY 'MODERN' CONCRETE TILE ON
- 38×25 SWD BATTENS ON
- UNDERLAY ON
- 50×150 SWD RAFTERS AT 600 OC
- CONTINUOUS VENTILATOR FIXED TO
  18 PLY FASCIA BOARD
- MARLEY 'PREMIER' GUTTER

UPSTAND
- 2 LAYER FIBREGLAS ROOFING ON
- 18 EXTERNAL GRADE DOUG. FIR PLY ON
- 50×75 SWD BATTENS AT 600 OC ON
- 140 BLOCKWORK

OVERHANG
- 2 LAYER FIBREGLAS ROOFING ON
- 18 EXTERNAL GRADE DOUG. FIR PLY ON
- 50×150 SWD CARCASSING
- 18 EXT. CLADDING GRADE DOUG. FIR PLY SOFFIT
- 75×6 GALV. STEEL SUPPORTS AT 1200 OC FIXED W.
  ANCHOR BOLTS TO BLOCKWORK
- 75 MM NAT. ANODISED ALUM. TRIM TO LEADING EDGE.

D1

Construction detail of the south facade (wall). Scale 1:10

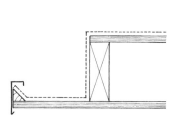

CEILING
- 12.5 PLASTERBD W.
- 3 SKIM COAT (EDGE + CORNER BEADS)
- 50×150 SWD BEARERS
- 150 FIBREGLAS INSULATION

WALL
- 18 EXT. CLADDING GRADE DOUG. FIR PLY ON
- 50×75 SWD BATTENS AT 600 OC ON
- 140 BLOCKWORK
- 45 STYROFOAM RIGID INSULATION
- 12.5 PLASTERBD ON FIRRING STRIPS W.
- 3 SKIM COAT (EDGE BEAD BOTTOM + ENDS)

D2

GROUND FLOOR
- 75 CONCRETE FLOOR W. A142 MESH
  POWERFLOAT FINISH, BUTTED EXPANSION
  JOINTS AS SHOWN ON PLAN 107/03
- VELTA UNDERFLOOR HEATING WITHIN 75 THICKNESS
- 40 STYROFOAM RIGID INSULATION
- 200 CONCRETE RAFT W. A142 MESH
- HEAVY DUTY POLYTHENE DPM
- 25 BLINDING LAYER
      HARDCORE

VERANDA
- 35×150 CEDAR W. TOP SURFACE PLANED ON
  50×150 SWD JOISTS AT 600 OC
  FIXED VIA JOIST HANGERS TO
  50×150 SWD WALL PLATE

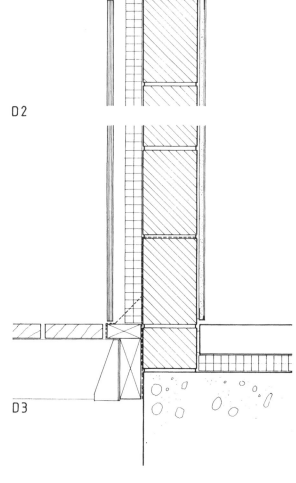

EXTERNAL WALL DETAIL
BURTON CROFT ROAD
CARUSO ST JOHN ARCHITECTS
071 609 9277

SCALE 1:5
DRWG: 107/50

D3

SOUTH FACADE
- 18 EXT. CLADDING GRADE DOUG. FIR PLY ON
  50x75 SWD BATTENS AT 600 OC ON
  140 BLOCKWORK
- 45 STYROFOAM RIGID INSULATION
- 12.5 PLASTERBD ON FIRRING W.
  3 SKIM COAT (EDGE BEAD BOTTOM + ENDS)
- 100x100x6 GALV. ANGLE FIXED W. ANCHOR BOLTS TO
  END OF BRICK CLADDING.
SLIDING DOOR
- NAT. ANODISED THERMALLY BROKEN
  ALUMINIUM FRAME
- 6·6·6 CLEAR TOUGHENED GLASS
- OPENING LINED WITH 30 MDF

Construction detail of the south facade
(corner and balcony). Scale 1:10

15 M/R MDF IN
BATHROOM

30

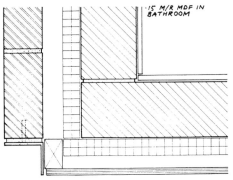
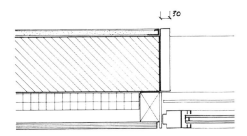

D1

100x100x6   6

EXTERNAL WALL DETAILS
BURTON CROFT ROAD
CARUSO ST JOHN ARCHITECTS
071 609 9277

SCALE 1:5
DRWG: 107/51

The house, roof of the garage and
entrance foyer enclose a small courtyard that Caruso and St. John have
paved with river stone. The south
facade, unseen from the street, is finished in fir panels rather than in brick.

D3

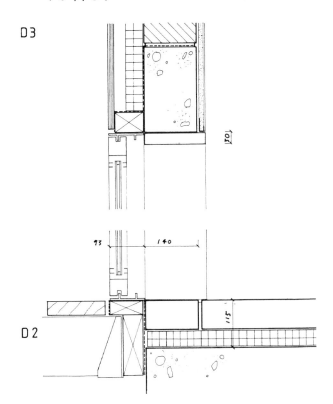

101

93   140

115

D2

Aranda, Pigem, Vilalta Arquitectes

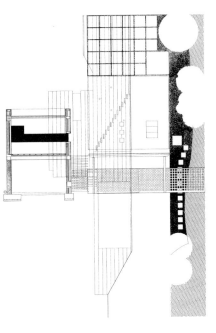

Architects: *Aranda, Pigem, Vilalta Arquitectes.*
Site: *Olot. Spain*
Collaborators: *Maria Tapies, Antonio Saez, Lagares S.A.*
Structure: *Saez and Ll. Moya*

Casa Margarida is a single-family house, designed to be used as a main residence. The aspects which characterise the project's locality are basically two; firstly, the orientation, which is favourable towards the street side and, secondly, the steep slope of this same street.

A white volume rises from behind the grey wall which borders the plot, it has a large opening protected by white, slatted blinds which filter the light. This two-storey block holds most of the spaces of the house. Another lower level, grey in color like the wall onto the street, is placed inside it. This second volume contains the kitchen, and on the lower level, the garage. The project includes only two more elements; a canopy which produces a horizontal line of shade, which divides the large opening of the main volume in two, and three vertical, metal tubes that correspond to the chimney. The structural forms are clear; the perimeter walls are load-bearing and have a metal framework.

The garden and the swimming pool can be found at the highest point of a flat area at street level. The entrance, on the other hand, is sited on the lowest part of the plot abutting onto the street. In this way, the access is not by the garden, but through the garage and some stairs which go up to the main floor. The garden is not, therefore, converted into a passing place, it is not discovered in the very first moment, rather, it possesses a private character and has a more flexible relationship with the interior.

The heart of the house is a double-height space over the dining room. The different spaces are organised around this emptiness, and they are characterised by the varying presence of natural light and by the visual play of reflections and transparencies.

The study of light led the architects to design complex elements, such as the canopy which runs the length of the white volume of the garden facade from one side to the other; however, it is interrupted in the moment that it meets up with the other lower volume. The upper part of the canopy is 0.5 inches (0.25 x 0.25) translucent, laminated glass, while the lower part is constructed from slats of bolondo wood, forming three planes with slightly different inclinations. The first layer of translucent glass diffuses the light, and the second one, made of fillets, produces the grating-effect shadows.

With the same care with which the architects configured the image of the building, they have constructed the exterior as a visual prolongation of the interior spaces.

Second floor. Scale:1/200

Basement. Scale:1/200

Ground floor. Scale:1/200

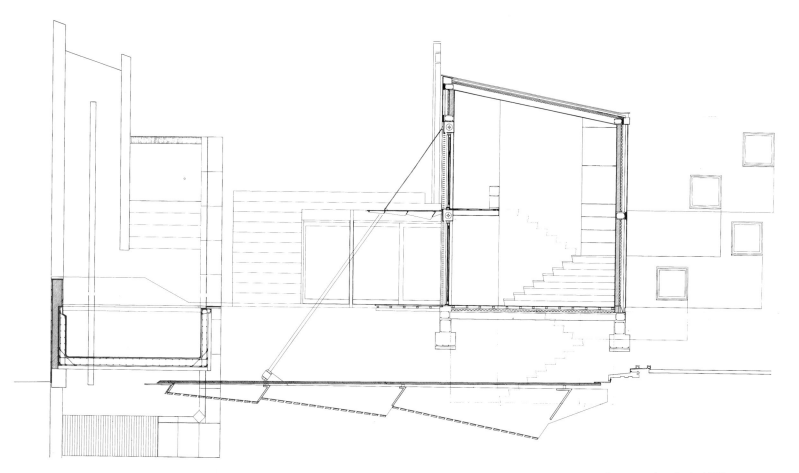

Cross section. Scale:1/200

Construction section of the kitchen module. Scale:1/50

1. 2 cm finish of San Vicente stone.
2. Artificial grass.
3. Protective layer of mortar.
4. Waterproofed material.
5. Polystyrene.
6. IPN wrought metal beams.
7. Slab clad in formica.
8. Reinforced concrete strip.
9. San Vicente stone.
10. Mortar.
11. 7 cm. block.
12. Air chamber.
13. 14cm. perforated brick wall.
14. Plaster.
15. A52b steel pillar, 80/9 mm. diameter.
16. 3 mm. stainless steel plate.
17. Reinforced concrete lintel.
18. Wooden rail.
19. 6 X 6mm. laminated glass.
20. PVC shutter.
21. Shutter with movable aluminum strips.
22. PVC sliding partition.
23. Aluminum guide.
24. 2 X 7cm. wood parquet.
25. Flanders pine strips.
26. Prestressed wrought beams and ceramic finishes.
27. Reinforced concrete containing wall.
28. Foundation.
29. Drainage tube.
30. White concrete paving.
31. Gravel.
32. PVC window.
33. White concrete in situ stairs.

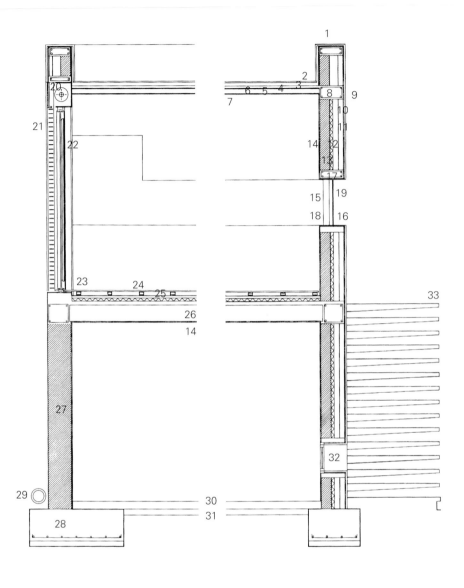

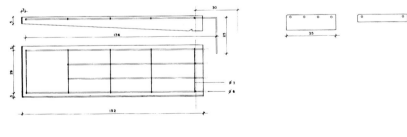

DETALLE ESCALERA   DETALL 3

Construction section of the main module.
Scale:1/50.

1. 2 cm. San Vicente stone finish.
2. Flat tile.
3. C. p. protective layer.
4. Polystyrene.
5. Prestressed wrought beams, ceramic finishes.
6. Plaster.
7. PVC gutter.
8. Mortar.
9. Stucco.
10. 7 cm. block.
11. Air chamber.
12. 14 cm. perforated brick wall.
13. Reinforced concrete band.
14. 2 cm. San Vicente stone plinth.
15. Waterproofed material.
16. Prestressed wrought beams, ceramic finishes.
17. Foundation.
18. Concrete support.
19. PVC shutter.
20. Shutter of movable aluminum strips.
21. PVC sliding partition.
22. Aluminum guide.
23 PVC sheet.
24. 2 X 7 cm. wood parquet.
25. Flanders pine strips.
26. IPN 160 wrought metal beams.
27. DM 16 mm. lacquered panel.
28. A-52 steel pillar, 80/9mm. diameter.
29. Stainless steel bar, 16mm. diameter.
30. 8mm. steel rib.
31. 8mm. longitudinal steel rib.
32. 6 X 6mm. translucent laminated glass.
33. 3 mm. stainless steel finish.
34. 6 cm. San Vicente stone finish.

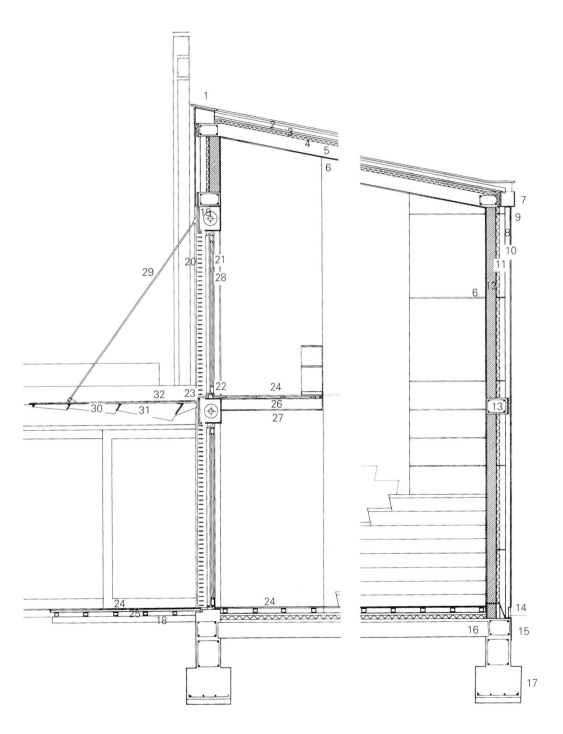

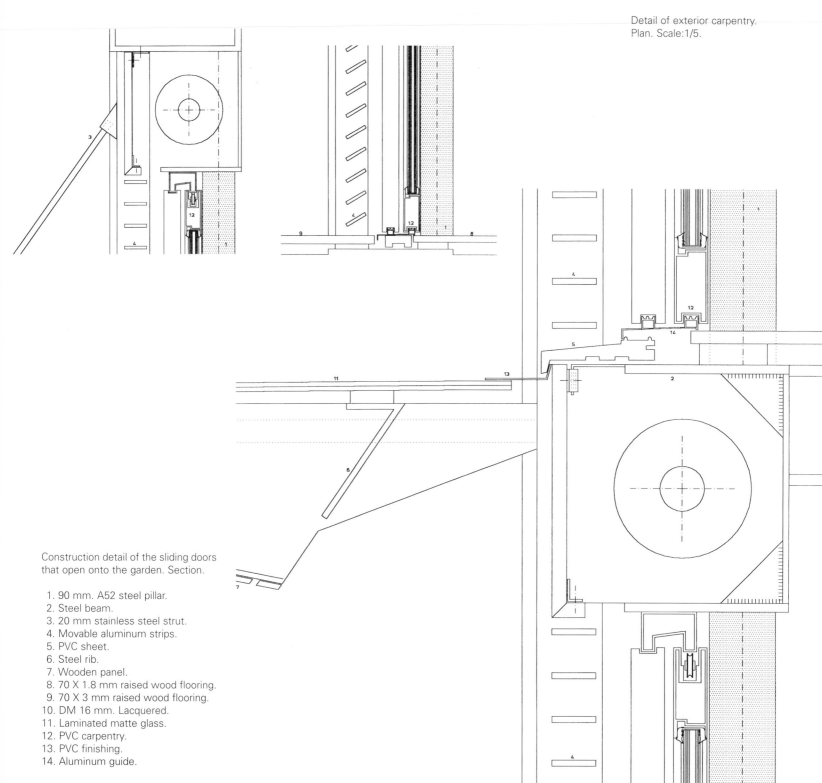

Construction detail of the sliding doors
that open onto the garden. Section.

1. 90 mm. A52 steel pillar.
2. Steel beam.
3. 20 mm stainless steel strut.
4. Movable aluminum strips.
5. PVC sheet.
6. Steel rib.
7. Wooden panel.
8. 70 X 1.8 mm raised wood flooring.
9. 70 X 3 mm raised wood flooring.
10. DM 16 mm. Lacquered.
11. Laminated matte glass.
12. PVC carpentry.
13. PVC finishing.
14. Aluminum guide.

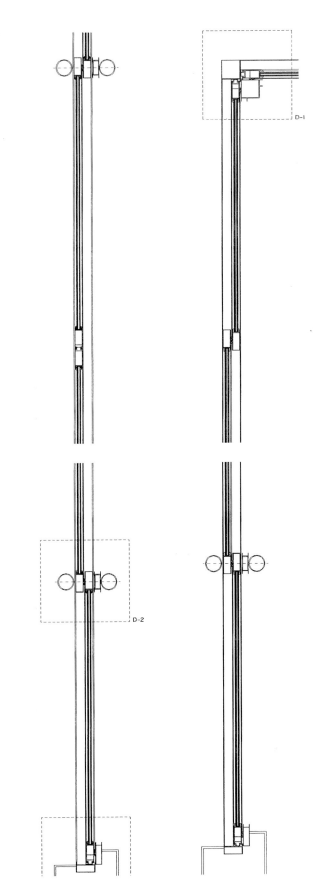

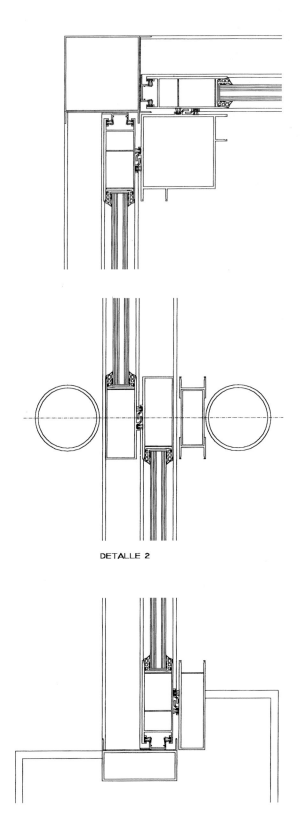

DETALLE 2

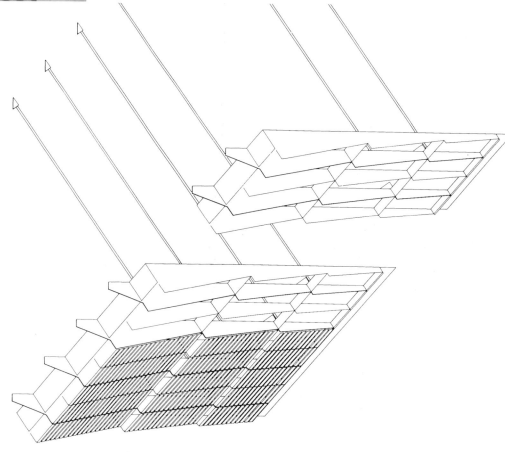

Detail of the pergola. Scale 1/2.

1. 32 mm anchoring bar.
2. Stainless steel bar, 16 mm diameter.
3. A-52 steel pillar, 80/9mm. diameter.
4. 32 mm. round transversal rib.
5. 8 mm. steel plate.
6. 8 mm. sheet metal rib.
7. 8 mm. sheet metal longitudinal rib.
8. Translucent 6 X 6 mm. laminated glass.
9. Neoprene joint.
10. 20 X 15 mm. aluminum angle.
11. Bolondo wood strip.
12. Fixing strip.
13. 3 mm. stainless steel finish.

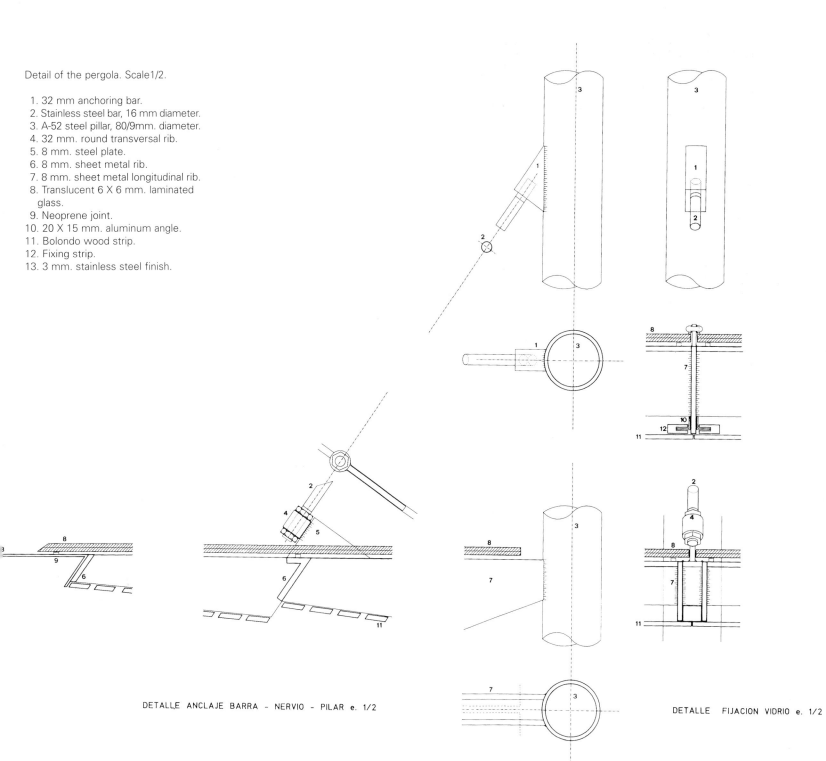

DETALLE ANCLAJE BARRA - NERVIO - PILAR e. 1/2

DETALLE FIJACION VIDRIO e. 1/2

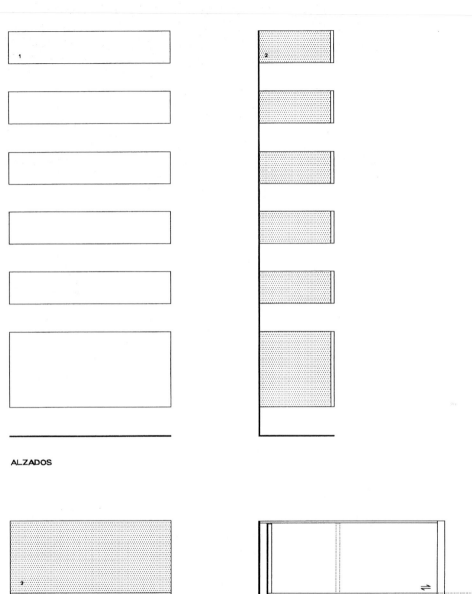

ALZADOS

PLANTA

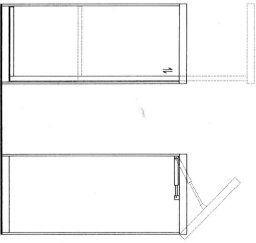

SECCION

Homage to Donald Judd furniture.

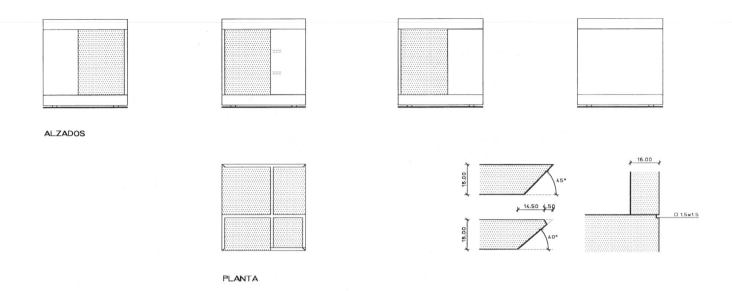

ALZADOS

PLANTA

Table.

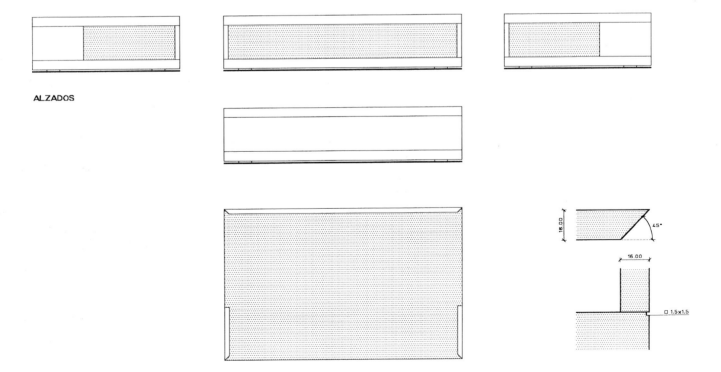

ALZADOS

PLANTA

House n. 14

Hiroshi Naito

Architects: *Hiroshi Naito.*
Site: *Tsukuba, Japan.*
Collaborator: *Tatsuo Yoshida.*

House No. 14 sits on a 1323m² site in an oak forest on the East slope of Mount Tsukuba. It is built of wood and has a simple and compact (200m²) square layout developed on two floors. The upper level is wider because of a projecting balcony running around its exterior. This greater mass on the top produces an effect of lightness as it seems to almost float, especially when viewed from the plot's highest point.

The owner needed a studio and a home large enough to accommodate the size of his works of art; hence, the workshop is on the ground floor and the dwelling is on the second.

Structurally simple, the house has four thick circular pillars in the center on which are supported dividing partitions which organize the spatial distribution. A skylight is situated in the roof's apex over the central area defined by the pillars.

The slope of the land makes it possible to access the home on the second floor, from the site's highest point, where the street is. From here the house is accessed via a bridge. On this floor the balcony entirely surrounds the house, enclosing the living room, kitchen and the bedrooms and forming a filter - a thick and accessible separation between interior and exterior. Thus, the line is blurred between surrounding nature and space belonging to the house. Sliding wood panels are situated on the perimeter.

Due to the project's limited budget, collaboration between the architect, the client and the builders was necessarily intense. Now, a few years later, the client seems satisfied with the result. Aside from a couple of minor mishaps, such as cracks in the skylight, the house remains in its original condition.

A small home has been built next to it for the client's father, who lost his home in the Kobe earthquake.

Hiroshi Naito's architecture is heavily influenced by traditional Japanese constructions.

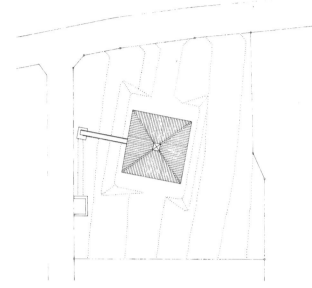

Site plan.

Cross section of the entrance walk-way.

The house lies on a plot between two slopes; nevertheless, it remains independent from the topography rather than being adapted to the terrain.

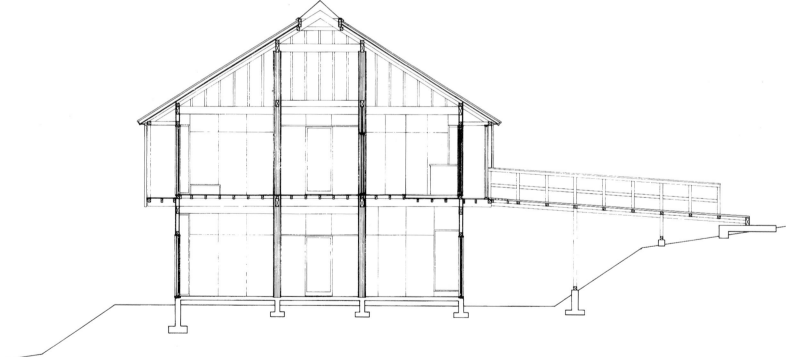

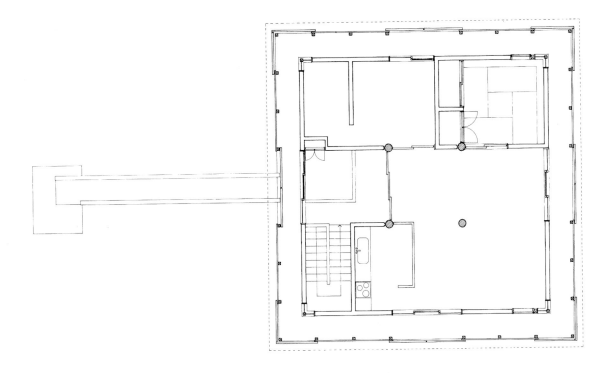

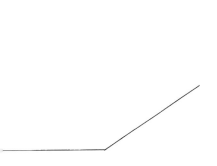

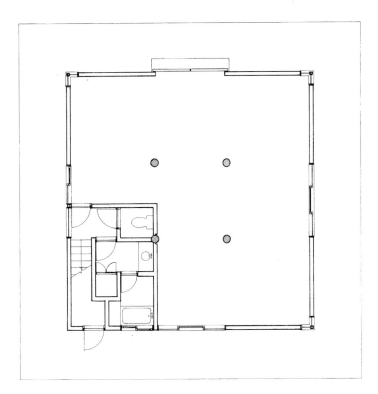

Second floor.

First floor.

The layout is a perfect square. Interior walls are aligned with four central roof-support pillars. The upper floor features a perimetral balcony surrounding the house.

Constructive axonometry. Throughout his professional career Hiroshi Naito has shown consummate knowledge of wood building techniques. This project as well as the Seafolk Museum are clear examples.

View of living room. Wood adds warmth to the atmosphere of the house.

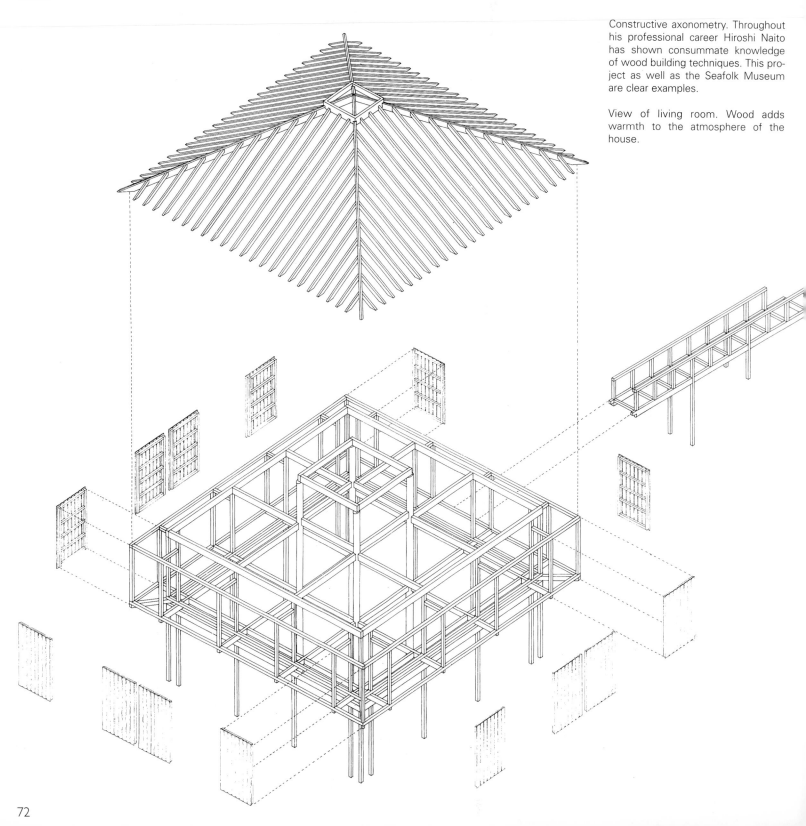

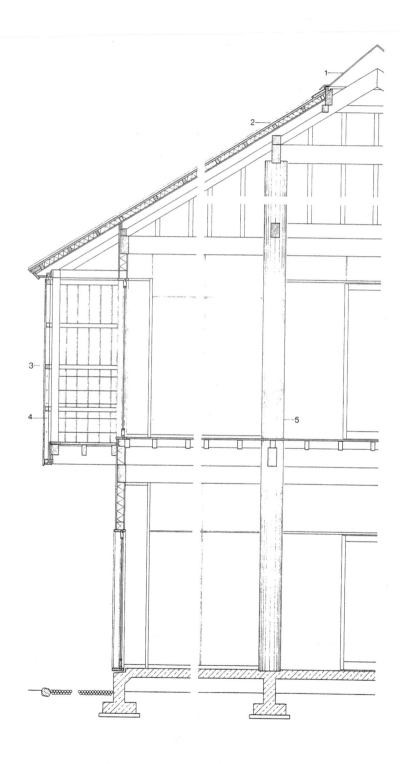

Constructive section.

1. Policarbonate sheet.
2. Roof:
   4 mm. metal plate.
   Layer of waterproofing.
   12 mm. wooden veneer.
   60 X 105 mm. wood beams.
3. Sliding doors.
4. Stainless steel cables of 3 mm.
   diameter.
5. Japanese cedar column of 300
   mm. diameter.
6. 6 mm. steel plate, folded for use
   as a guide.
7. Immovable glass.
8. Wall.
   12 mm. cedar panel.
   105 mm. insulation.
   6 mm. wooden veneer.
9. 105 X 105 mm. pine strips.
10. Sliding-glass door.
11. 12 mm. cedar panel.
12. Ceiling channel sealed with
    Perspex.

Constructive detail of upper level hallway.

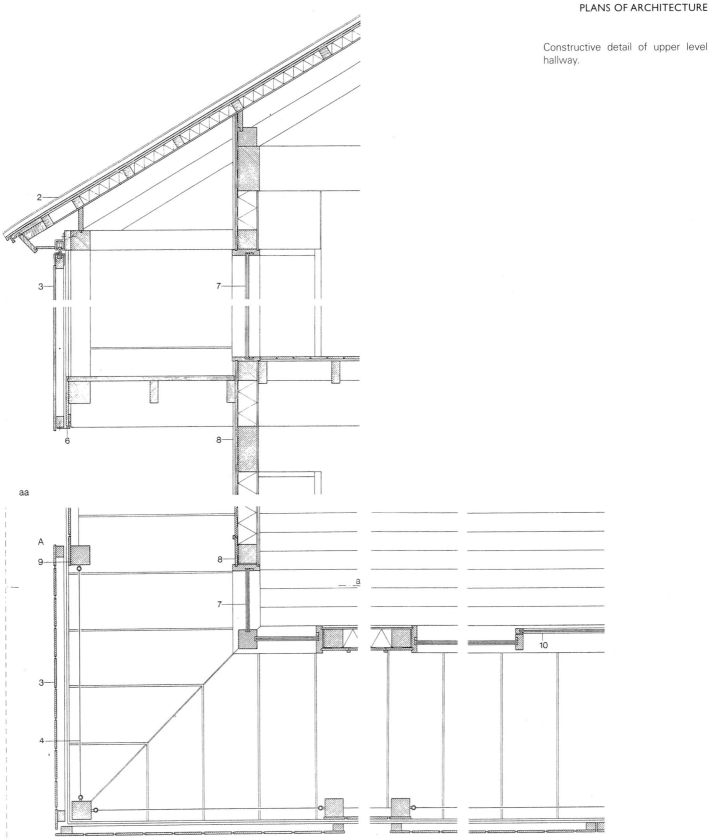

View of hallway.

Roof detail.

Volker Giencke

Architect: *Volker Giencke*
Site: *Graz. Austria*

The house and workshop were built just below the summit of Mount Rosenberg on a plot which was once an orchard. The workshop is almost completely below ground and its glazed frontal facade exactly reproduces the incline of the slope on which it lies. The single-family home is constructed longitudinally over the workshop. The two bodies lie on a southwest-northeast axis although slightly angled toward each other. Vehicle access is through a terrace which also serves as a parking lot for workshop personnel. The parking area for the family's cars is on the site's highest point on the north angle. From here a curved path leads to the terrace in front of the house.

The workshop: The glass roof is 35 X 8 m. Lateral projections reinforce the joining axis which crosses the volume along the length from north to south. The transversal section is a 2.5m deep underground trapezium which opens onto the main area of the workshop by way of circular columns. The entrance is from the north part of the parking lot where there is a raised (70 cm.) path that joins the workshop to the "Cage of Wind", a room used as a wardrobe during the winter months. An arched ramp of cedar crosses the central work space and leads to the library and archives, the kitchen, service area and the "Emergencies and Catastrophes Room". Above the latter space is the heating equipment which consists of an underground water pumping system which takes advantage of the heating energy of deep reserves (200 m.). On both sides of the workshop, movable facades of double insulating glass (2 X 2m) allow an extension of the workshop in summer through a strut and counterweight system which achieves an opening similar to that of a garage door. With the aim of increasing shade, white sails have been stretched (via a system of struts and rails) across the inclined glass facade.

The house: The frame is a 9 m^2 modular structure composed of steel square sections (120 mm^2). The height is 6m with a width of 39m. The upper level contains the inhabitable spaces while the lower is designed for winter use. The living rooms are located on the south and north ends, both of them enjoying ample light and ventilation. Kitchen and water storage are behind these while the children's' and guests' rooms are between the living rooms and kitchen. The dining room, cozy yet appropriate for work, features a folding ladder which leads to a loft. The rest of the layout is an open air terrace.

The house lies on Mount Rosenberg surrounded by the hilly landscape characteristic of Graz.

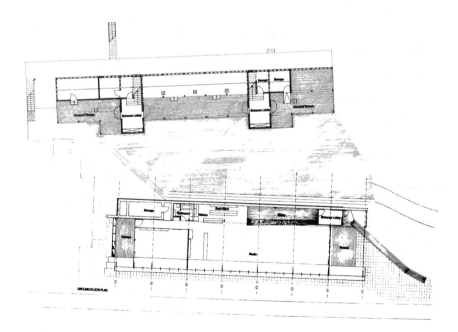

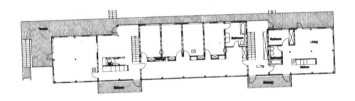

Workshop and ground-floor layouts.

Second floor layout.

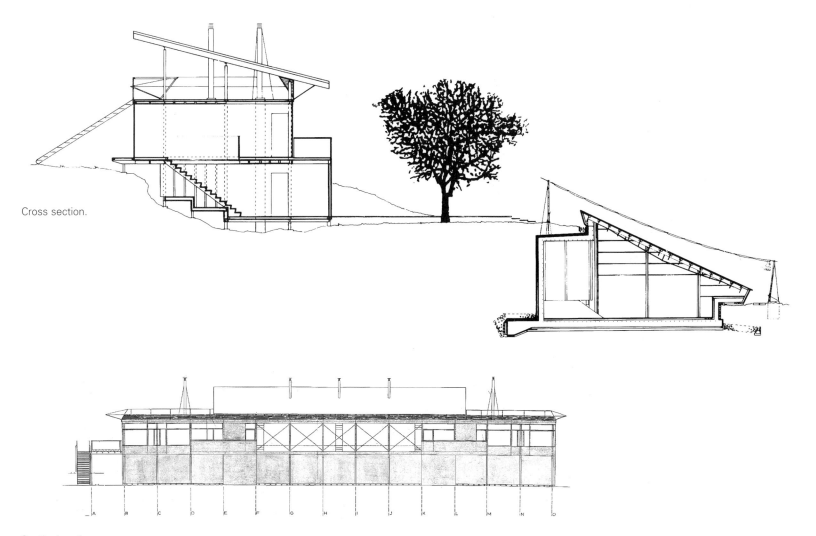

Cross section.

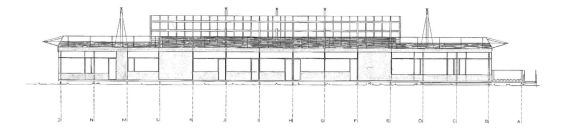

South elevation.

North elevation.

The house is built with 120 X 120 mm steel sections which form a 3 X 3 m mesh. The width of the house is 6 m. (two modules), the length is 39 m. (12 modules).

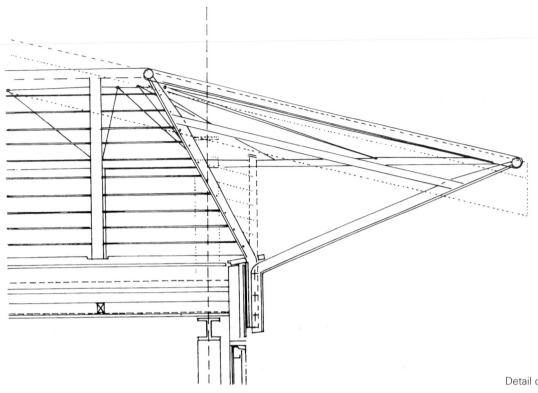

Detail of guard rail on the roof.

The amount of constructed exterior spaces is one of the notable features of this house. On the roof as well as on the ground floor they are protected by pergolas and trellises, thereby obtaining a cozier and more comfortable atmosphere.

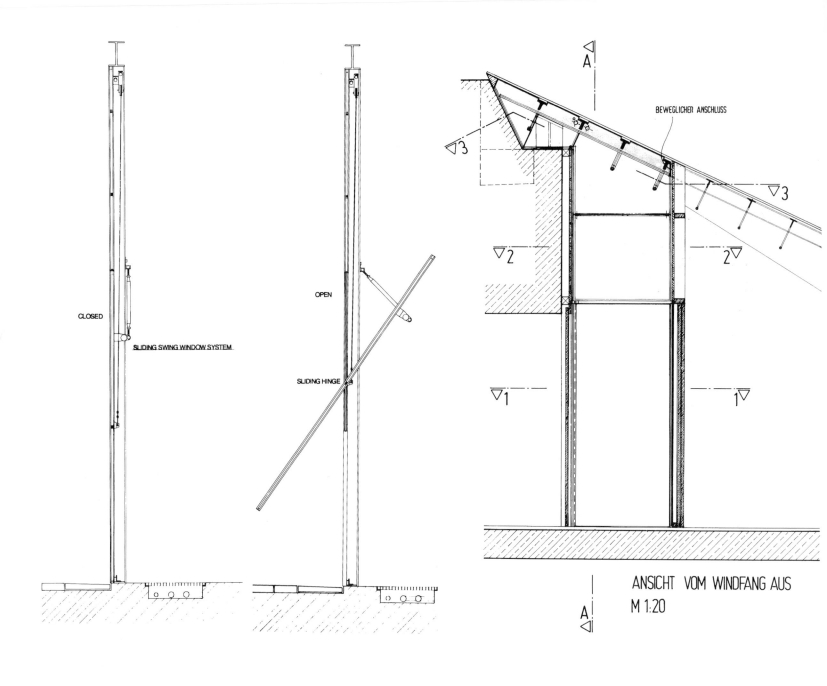

CLOSED

SLIDING SWING WINDOW SYSTEM

OPEN

SLIDING HINGE

BEWEGLICHER ANSCHLUSS

ANSICHT VOM WINDFANG AUS
M 1:20

Detail of the windows.

Cross section of the workshop's glass roof.

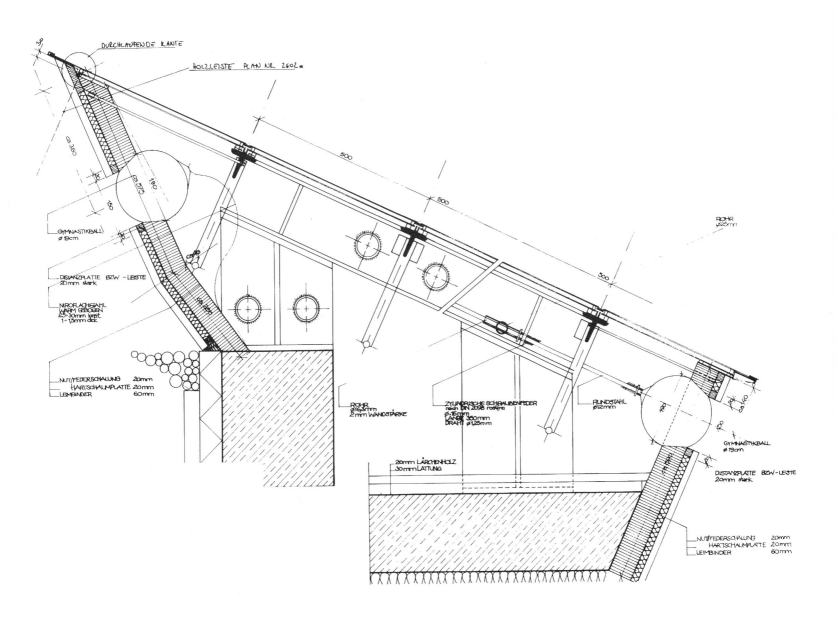

White nautical sails have been stretched over the inclined glass facade through a system of rails and tie rods. These sails form soft, undulating surfaces, contrasting with the structure of the roof.

Constructive detail of the roof of the workshop.

Helio Olga House

Marcos Acayaba

Architect: *Marcos Acayaba*
Site: *Sao Paulo. Brazil.*
Collaborators: *Mauro Halluili, Edison Hiroyama, Tania Shirakawa*
Structure, Appliances and Construction: *Helio Olga de Souza, jr.*

This project exemplifies one of the possible relationships which a house can establish with the terrain when the latter presents a slope that exceeds 45 degrees. It was not in vain that it was conceived as a prototype for very uneven localities, using prefabricated structural elements. Vehicle access is via the upper level. Marcos Acayaba could not resist the temptation to overfly the cliff.

The project consists of two parts: a tower in form of a «T» and a private terrace which includes the swimming pool and the garage. The terrace, which forms the access plane, rests on the horizontal limit of the plot. The four-storey tower is set on concrete props set into the slope, so that one extreme of the upper floor rests on the terrace. The disposition of the tower, perpendicular to the topographic lines, and its leading to the terrace, can cause the project to be thought of as the beginning of a bridge: the transparency of the upper floor and its condition of a horizontal plane in mid-air, convert going through the dwelling's main room into a stroll along a platform suspended in the air.

There are six props, with a depth of 60 feet, which protrude from the surface to delimit the two squares of 11 feet that make up the supporting base for the tower. This perimeter is repeated for the two lower floors, the northern half (which is the optimum orientation in the southern hemisphere) corresponds to the rooms, and in the southern half are the services and the staircase. The middle floor has three times the surface and assigns the same functional division to its modules. Finally, the main or upper floor has two more modules on each side, near the terrace.

It consists of an overhanging structure of pillars and wooden beams forming a volumetric reticle whose planes are braced with steel cables in both diagonals. Its symmetry makes it stable by compensation. By minimising the supporting surface, the foundation costs were reduced and the original profile was kept intact.

The exterior is enlightening. The house's façades show and explain its interior workings, its construction and the concepts of its structure. While the metallic guys cross in front and the wooden joists appear outside, the blinds combine with the partitions in geometric modules, thus identifying each one of the rooms.

The plane of the roof overhangs the whole, and incorporates details which convert the work of engineering into poetry. Four metal tubes hang in the air in the lateral extremes: rainwater is scattered by the wind, re-affirming the impartiality of the terrain.

In a context conditioned by the land, what stands out are colors, materials and, above all, the expressive force of a form resolved with technical-constructive resources normally reserved for other ends.

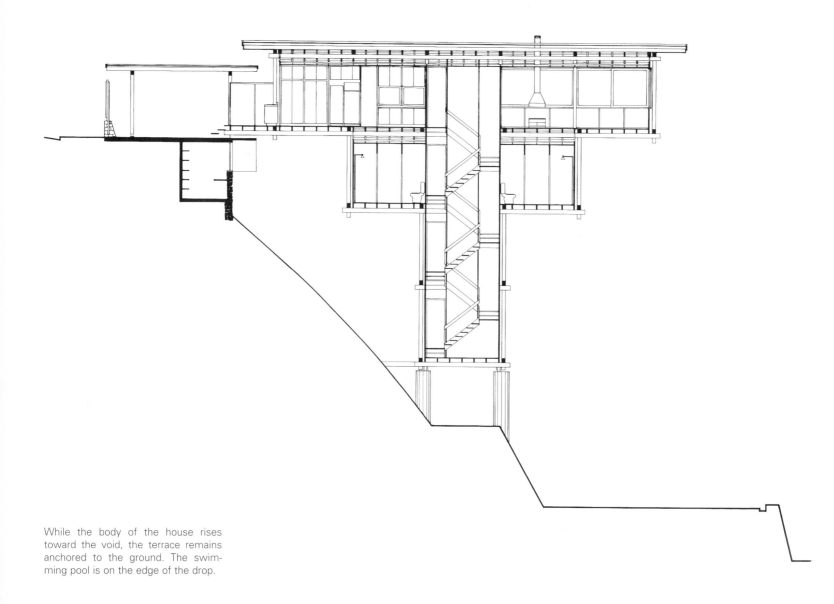

While the body of the house rises toward the void, the terrace remains anchored to the ground. The swimming pool is on the edge of the drop.

Following page:

Upper level. Level 0.00

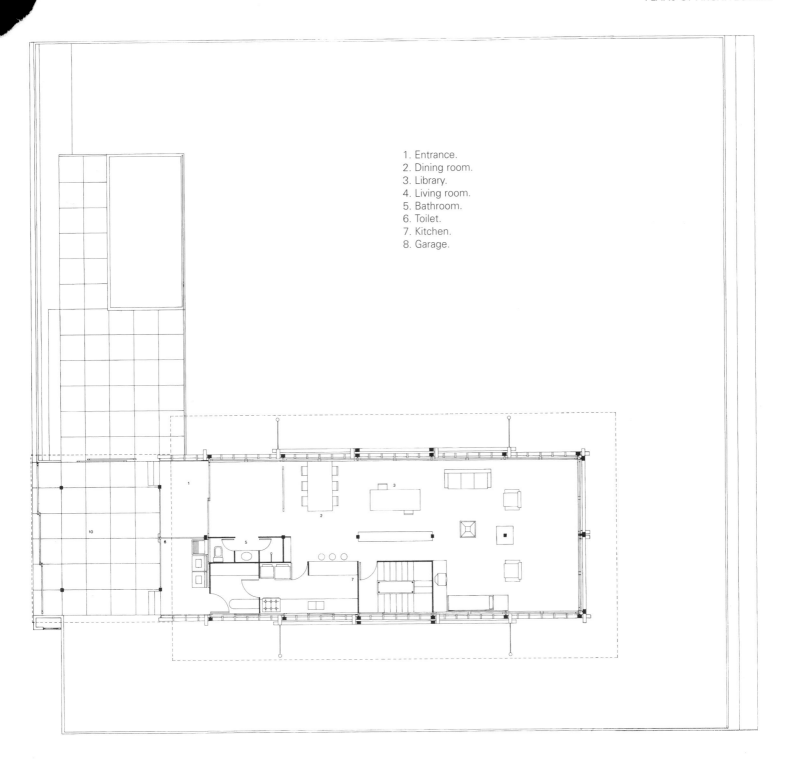

1. Entrance.
2. Dining room.
3. Library.
4. Living room.
5. Bathroom.
6. Toilet.
7. Kitchen.
8. Garage.

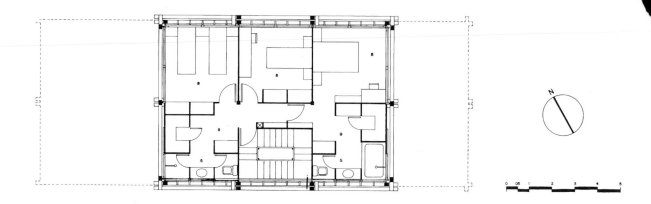

Floor at level -3.3

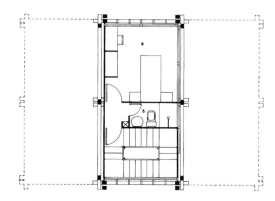

Floor at level -6.6

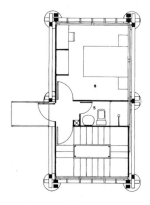

Floor at level -9.9

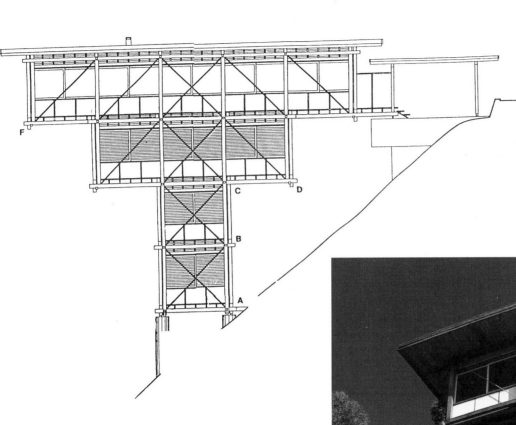

Wooden beams and joints are superimposed to form overhangings, leaving the space between them open to the view. The majority of the facade modules form sills of three white panels and wood carpentry that divides its upper portion into two. Drainpipes are suspended from the roof overhang.

Lateral elevation.

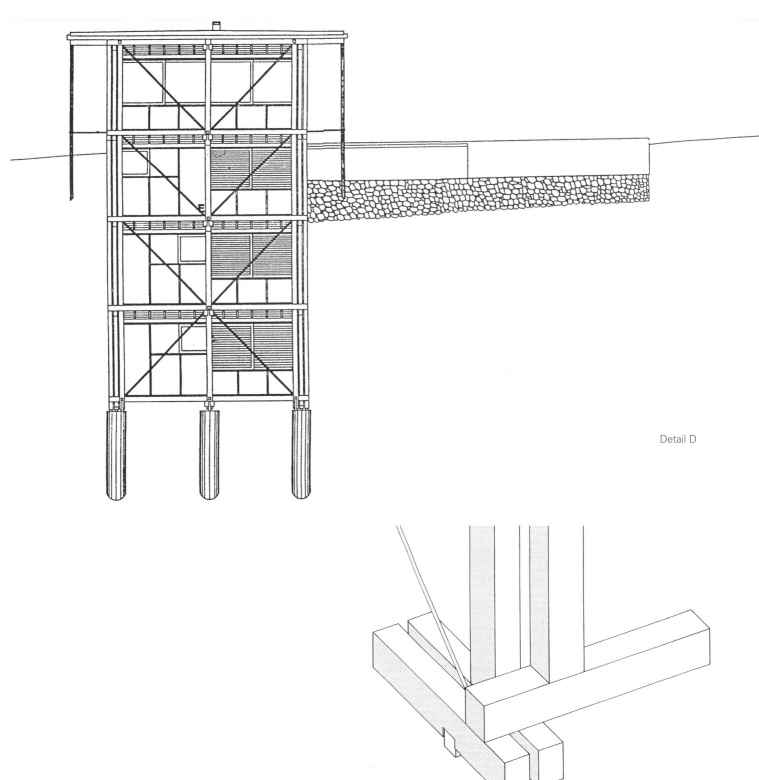

Detail D

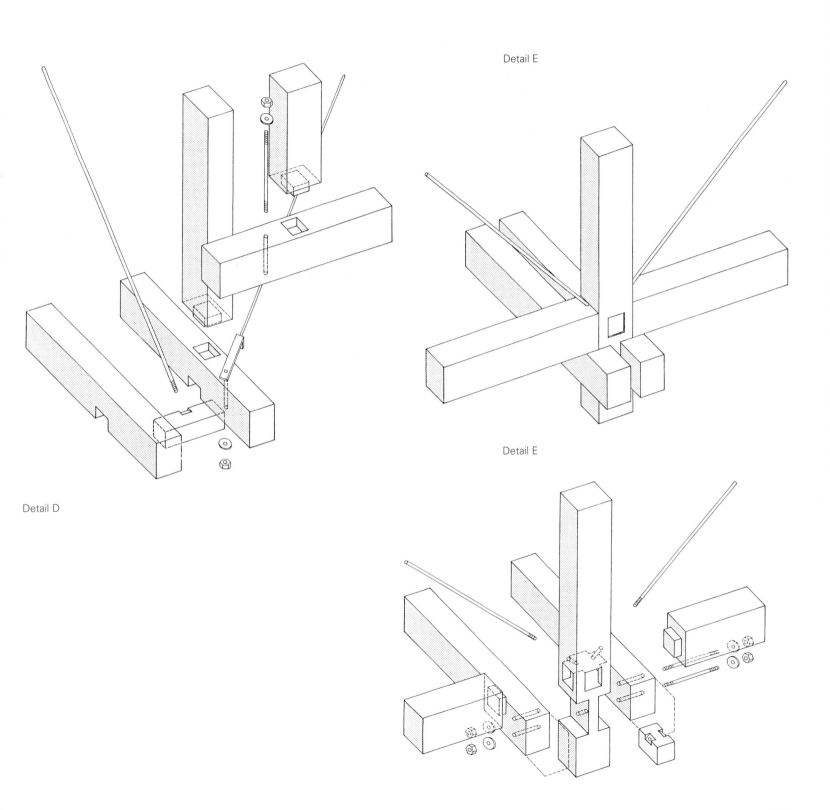

Detail E

Detail E

Detail D

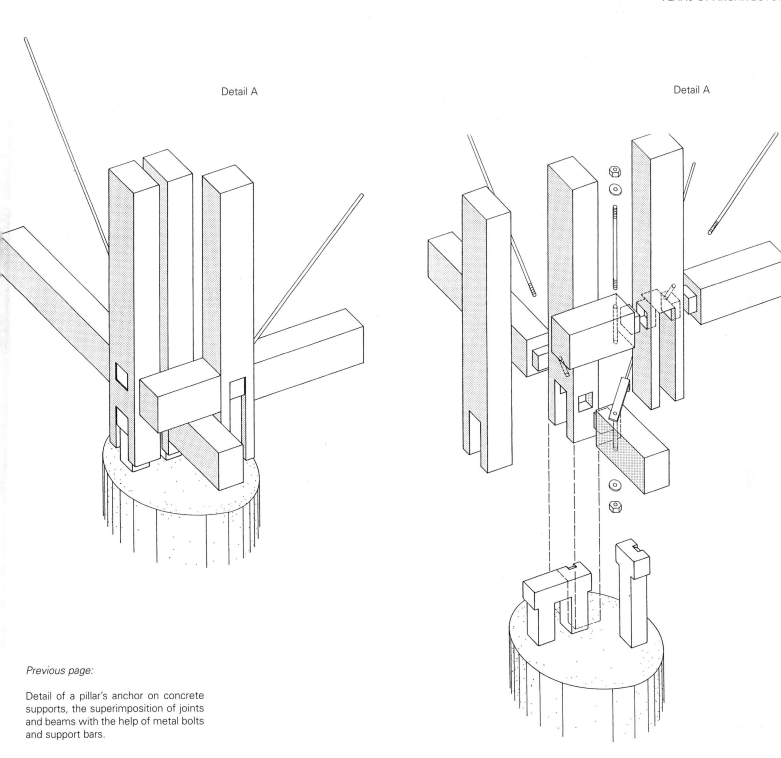

Detail A

Detail A

Previous page:

Detail of a pillar's anchor on concrete supports, the superimposition of joints and beams with the help of metal bolts and support bars.

Detail B

Detail B

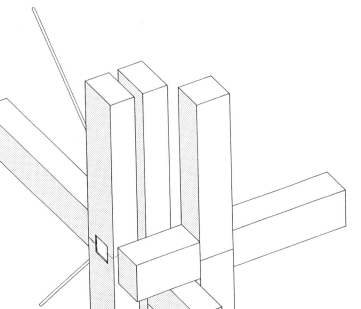

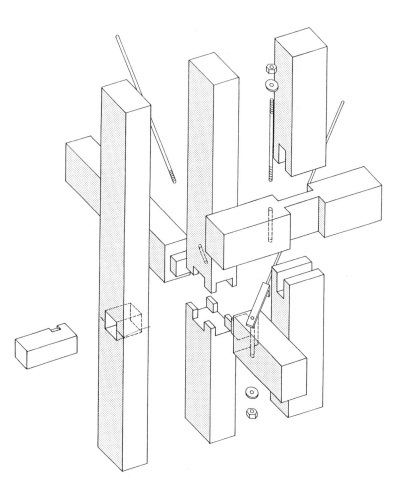

Detail C

Detail C

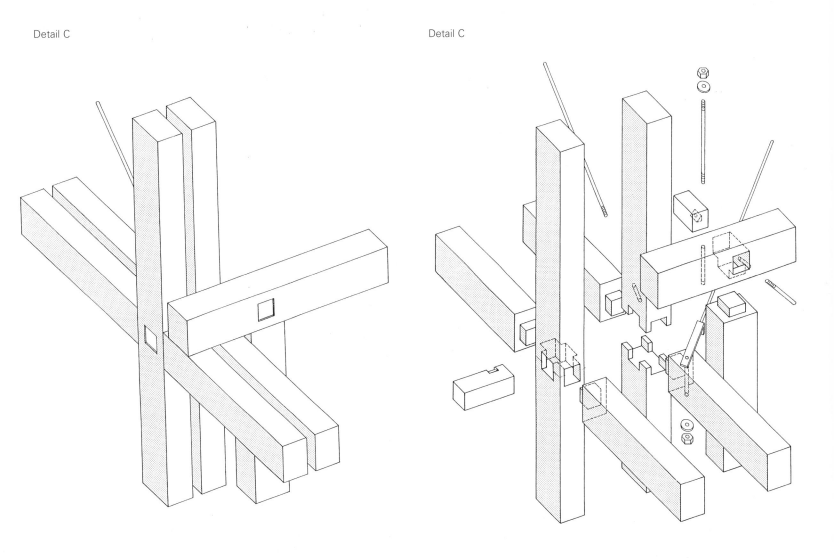

Aronoff House

Eric Owen Moss

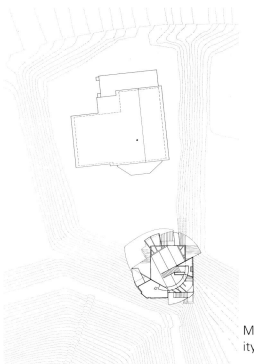

Architect: *Eric Owen Moss*
Site: *Santa Monica. California (USA)*
Project Architect: *Scott M. Nakao*
Structural Engineer: *Robert Lawson Estructural*
Mechanical Engineer: *Greg Tchamitchian. AEC SYSTEMS*

The property stretches north-west of the existing house and down a slope to the Santa Monica Reserve, a beautiful wooded area extending for several miles, protected in perpetuity from development.

The new guest house is a toy for its owners, their employees, guests and children. The building can be climbed on, examined, and used as a viewing platform. The building location and the configuration of floors and windows maximizes spectacular and diverse views of the forest. The project - combining studio, office, and a private apartment - is positioned at the transition from flat to sloping portion of the site, adjacent to the south-west property line, exploiting the view without interrupting views from the existing main house. The position of the new house on the site also allows clear visibility and access from the street for those who come to it directly to do business.

The project contains 3 floors: the top level studio/executive offices for the owners; an office floor at grade for a business with three employees, and a separate apartment below for an elderly father. The roof, designed as a stepped bleacher/deck with open and covered areas, is oriented to the view of the Reserve area and the San Fernando Valley. It is accessible from all levels via a stair that runs along the perimeter of the house. It is also accessible internally, directly from the third floor.

The middle (grade level) is the office floor for the three employees, used during the work day in conjunction with owners' offices on the top floor. The apartment at the lowest level has elevator access, a covered deck area, and an open patio. All levels may be accessed from the middle level lobby or from the exterior.

Rather than stacking floors as a building steps to acknowledge a hillside profile, the guest house emerges from a conical cut dug at the edge of the hill. The project - secured at the edge - combines sphere and cube, neither quite legible.

Placed precariously at the top of a slope yet stabilized by the conical cut threatening to roll as a sphere and re-anchored by the cube, the guest house is a stable instability.

Site plan.

6/7 Arnoff
9:00 pm

6/27/91
7:00 pm

(6-27)

vertical ext

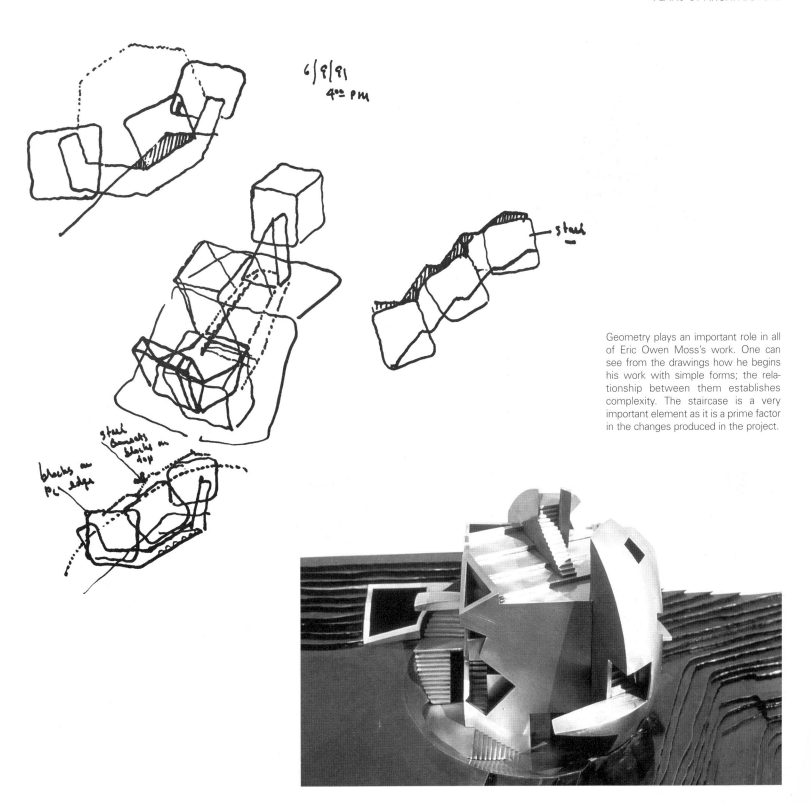

6/9/91
4:00 PM

steel

Geometry plays an important role in all of Eric Owen Moss's work. One can see from the drawings how he begins his work with simple forms; the relationship between them establishes complexity. The staircase is a very important element as it is a prime factor in the changes produced in the project.

Wall detail.

Section. Scale 1:100

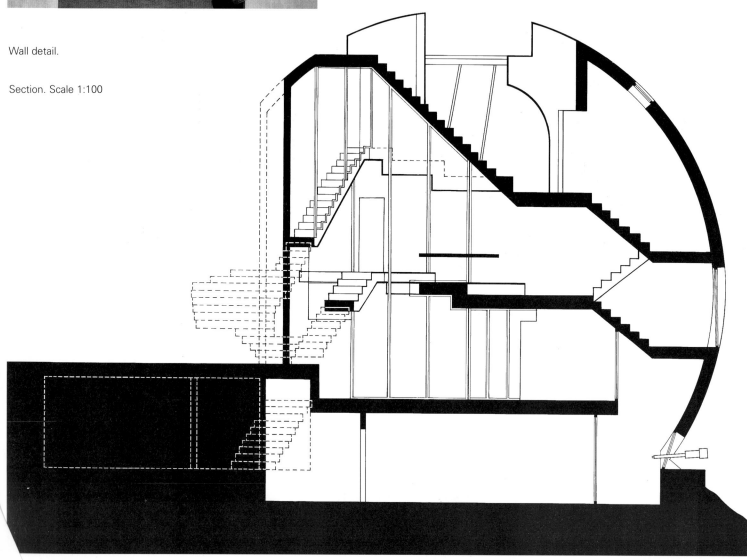

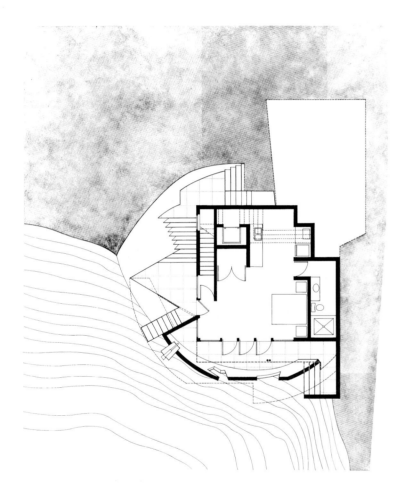

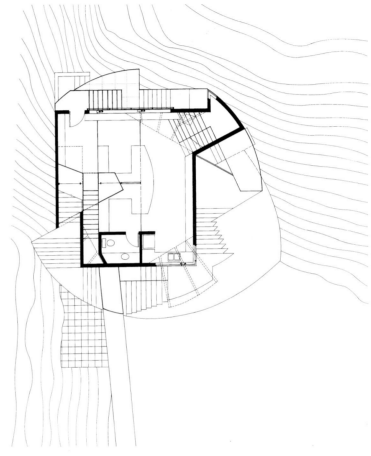

Ground floor. Scale 1:200

Second floor. Scale 1:200

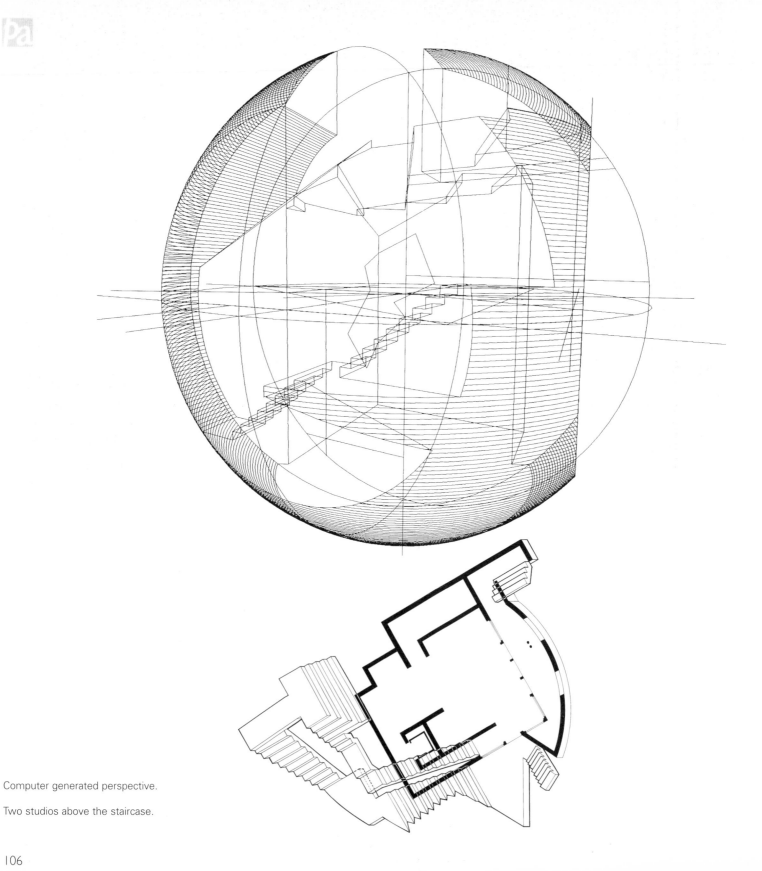

Computer generated perspective.

Two studios above the staircase.

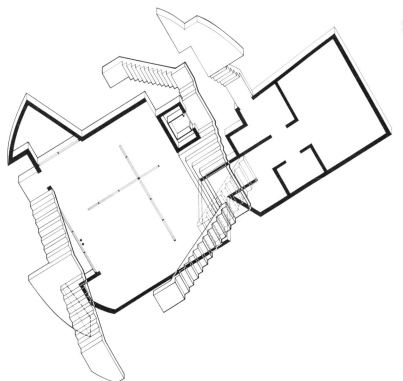